OVERTIME!
*A 20th Century
Sports Odyssey*

OTHER BOOKS BY PETER SCHWED

Turning the Pages: An Insider's Story of Simon & Schuster 1924–1984

*Hanging in There!: How to Resist Retirement from Life and
Avoid Being Put Out to Pasture*

Test Your Tennis I.Q.

God Bless Pawnbrokers

The Serve and the Overhead Smash

Sinister Tennis: How to Play Against and With Left-Handers

AS COLLABORATOR
The Education of a Woman Golfer (with Nancy Lopez)

AS COEDITOR
The Fireside Book of Tennis (with Allison Danzig)
Great Stories from the World of Sport (with Herbert Warren Wind)

AS COMPILER
The Cook Charts

OVERTIME!

A 20th Century Sports Odyssey

PETER SCHWED

BEAUFORT BOOKS
PUBLISHERS
New York

Library of Congress Cataloging-in-Publication Data

Schwed, Peter.
    Overtime!: a 20th century sports odyssey.

    1. Sports.   2. Athletes.   I. Title.
GV707.S35   1987   796   87-14486
ISBN 0-8253-0438-5

Published in the United States by Beaufort Books Publishers, New York

Designed by Irving Perkins Associates, Inc.

Printed in the U.S.A.   First Edition

10   9   8   7   6   5   4   3   2   1

FOR MY ANTONIA
who lovingly accepted my passion for sport
like the good sport she is

Contents

INTRODUCTION ix

1. GHOST STORY 3
   The alter egos of Willie Mays and Leo Durocher

2. THE SPLENDID SPLINTER 11
   Inside Ted Williams

3. SWABBING THE DECK IN NANCY'S NAVY 18
   *Life with Nancy Lopez. Also with Tommy Armour and
   Big Bill Tilden*

4. A SCATTERING OF SPORTS TIPS 26
   On tennis, golf, football, baseball, track, and poker

5. ROD LAVER AND THE FATES 36
   My chance for immortality

6. SORRY ABOUT THAT! 40
   Chris Evert meant well

7. THE GOLDEN BEAR 45
   Jack Nicklaus sinks a putt

8. THE 1889 SUPER BOWL 53
   A New York City holiday for the Princeton-Yale game

9. THE WORLD SERIES WITHOUT TELEVISION 59
   Giants vs. Yankees: a tale of two schoolboys in 1921

10. MY OLD MAN 66
    Winner take all

11. THE SPORT OF KINGS 76
    Horse players die broke

CONTENTS

12. THE AWFUL TRUTH   80
    The big leagues never wanted me

13. A BIRD IN THE HAND   83
    The glorious days of badminton

14. LOSERS WEEPERS?   90
    The triumphs of the defeated

15. OH, TO BE IN ENGLAND!   104
    A tennis player's problems across the Atlantic

16. MANY MILES TO GO   109
    Bill Bonthron, Glenn Cunningham, and Jack Lovelock

17. FREDDY AND LE SPORT   118
    A better funnyman than athlete

18. PUT UP OR SHUT UP   120
    A very frustrating story

19. THE INCREDIBLE BROWNIE   127
    No one else ever did what Mary K. Browne did

20. EVERY DOG HAS ITS DAY   133
    The year when chess took over the sports page

21. SOME LIKE IT HOT—AND SOME DO NOT!   139
    *Twenty-five laps around the track in the broiling
    100° sun*

22. "WHAT'S A DROPKICK, GRANDPA?"   148
    A question for archaeologists

23. ETERNAL TRIANGLES   152
    Willie Hoppe won 51 world titles over 47 years

24. THE LITTLE RED NOTEBOOK   160
    How clerical aptitude can keep your tennis game going

25. THE ONE AND ONLY ABSOLUTE BEST   164
    The all-time sports champion without any argument

26. COLOR MY EYEGLASSES ROSY   171
    Some modest proposals about rules

27. VETERAN'S VAUDEVILLE   179
    A man can dream, can't he?

Introduction

In sports, overtime is the period of play that goes past the regular time limits of a game to decide a tie. In using the word as the title of this book, I've given it a somewhat different meaning: a time to reflect back, after a lifelong obsession with sports, upon the incidents and people that made that world so fascinating for me. Not only have I had interesting or dramatic or funny experiences myself, but for the major portion of my business career I also was the editor for a great many books by famous athletes, and so I got to know them pretty well and garnered personal yarns about them that no one has ever heard before. Just to give you an idea of the cast of characters who make at least cameo appearances in these pages, a dozen of them picked at random and listed alphabetically are Tommy Armour, Bill Bonthron, Leo Durocher, Rod Laver, Chris Evert, Nancy Lopez, Willie Mays, Jack Nicklaus, Arnold Palmer, Branch Rickey, Big Bill Tilden, and Ted Williams, and there are many more of comparable note.

In my youth, for a boy to become a sports freak was as natural as the change of seasons. Boys didn't have to be taught about the world of sports or seduced into becoming interested in it—they simply became a part of it as easily as they took to cold cereal. After all, this was the period that has become known as the "Golden Age of Sport"—the 1920's. Everyone was distressingly role-conscious then, so girls were pretty well excluded from the fellowship of sportsmen. It took a truly unique event, like Gertrude Ederle's swim across the English Channel or the fabulous Suzanne Lenglen–Helen Wills tennis match at Cannes to capture the public's full interest in any women's sports activities. If I had had a sister, I doubt that she would have paid much attention to the daily conversations that my father, brothers, and I had about a constant flow of heroes such as Babe Ruth, Red Grange, Bobby Jones, Bill Tilden, or Paavo Nurmi. I know that my mother, as loving as she was, certainly didn't. But my father was loaded with stunning and almost hard-to-believe sports stories, to which I listened avidly and which I passed down to my children; today I keep the torch aflame by adding them to my own anecdotes that I tell my children and, heaven forgive me, my grandchildren. It is written that the iniquities of the father shall be visited upon the children unto the third and fourth generations; that seems to be true in my family's case. The fact is that I include in this book an unusually romantic and charming football story my father told me about "the 1889 Super Bowl" because it tells the reader something about the background that turned me into the sports freak I became, which in turn made ardent sports fans of my boys. My daughters went to school and college before women were able to enjoy the sports opportunities they have today, so they didn't grow up in our male locker-room atmosphere, but these days they, too, take a lively interest in several sports and have their heroines and heroes in the world.

In 1819 William Hazlitt wrote as part of his stirring tribute to John Cavanagh* at the time of that great champion's death: "It may be said that there are things of more importance than striking a ball against a wall—there are things indeed that make more noise and do as little good, such as making war and peace, making speeches and answering them, making verses and blotting them, making money and throwing it away." The essay goes on not only to extol the genius of Cavanagh's artistry but also to celebrate the joy that playing and watching sports can afford. Those of us today who have always been captivated by sports but are a little ashamed of the fascination it holds for us while perilous matters in the larger

*Cavanagh's game, extremely popular in England at the time, was the predecessor of handball and was very much like it. It was known as "fives."

world should be our overriding concern, can take comfort from Hazlitt's words. They indicate that more than 150 years ago sports were a major preoccupation of many people, even though at just about the same time the fate of Europe had been decided at Waterloo, the British prime minister had been assassinated right in the House of Commons, and the life of Beethoven, the greatest of composers, seemed to be threatened in midcareer by his becoming completely deaf. Despite such events, then as now people did indeed place importance on playing and watching games, and reading and talking about them.

OVERTIME!

A 20th Century
Sports Odyssey

CHAPTER 1

Ghost Story

*The alter egos of Willie Mays
and Leo Durocher*

I spent a good part of my publishing career pursuing ghosts. By that I mean ghostwriters. As an editor who was bemused by sports, I signed up a great many stars who had every qualification to be the authors of successful books except for one—they couldn't write their way out of a paper bag. Or wouldn't, because—let's face it—the money that's likely to be earned from a book's publication is pin money compared to what notable athletes make each year.

It's not pin money for most writers, however, and, apart from such considerations, ghostwriting a book with an athlete, who may well be something of an idol to a sports-minded author, has its decided attractions. Of the more than 50 sports books I handled at Simon & Schuster, the overwhelming majority required the collaboration of a professional writer, and that's why I pursued so many ghosts. Two of the best were Charlie Einstein and Ed Linn, both baseball mavens and admirably equipped to moonlight at ghostwriting when they weren't turning out their own articles and books.

Although Simon & Schuster published most of Charlie Einstein's books and I was not only his editor but also his close friend, he ghosted a wonderful baseball book that got away from us. That was *Willie's Time,* the Willie Mays story, which was published by another house that bid more for it than S&S was willing to risk. It was a mistake on our part, for we had had great success with the Fireside Baseball Books that Charlie had put together, we knew how good he was, and how could anyone pick a more engaging and heroic baseball figure than Willie? The book turned out to be a real winner, from both a commercial and a literary standpoint: it become a best-seller and was nominated for the National Book Award, a rare honor for a sports book.

Charlie has kept up his friendship with Willie, and every time we get together for lunch I ask him if he has a new Willie Mays story to tell me, knowing full well that as one of the hemisphere's great raconteurs, he will oblige. A bit further on I'll tell you one of his stories, but first a few words about Charlie Einstein.

His very first job on a sports desk was as a rewrite man with the International News Service, where in later years he became a nationally known feature writer and columnist. At that time his editor was known for two things: the excellent column he wrote, and his occasional intense drinking binges that made him miss deadlines. One day, only about a week after Charlie was hired, the editor called in on the telephone, obviously from a bar, and barked, "Gimme Einstein!"

The telephone operator, like Charlie, had been recently employed by INS; while she knew the names of the bosses, she had no idea of who "Einstein" might be, but the caller on the other end of the wire sounded very positive and very insistent. So she pulled out a sheet of telephone numbers with which she'd been supplied, listing the private numbers of celebrities whom INS might want to reach. Sure enough, there she found "Einstein," whose first name seemed to be Albert and who had a number in Princeton, New Jersey.

She rang through, and the great propounder of the Theory of Relativity, who invariably answered the telephone himself since he received so few calls, picked up the receiver and said, "Hello?"

Back came a staccato snarl. "Einstein? Take this down! The

Cubs finally put together two hits back to back in the seventh inning but by that time they were so far out of things that . . .". Einstein sat there listening, bemused, tried to interject a few words in German, and when the caller slammed down his receiver at the end of his report without any sign-off, we can only guess that Albert Einstein gently replaced his receiver and went back to mathematical calculations or whatever else he had been doing when this mysterious gibberish interrupted him.

Meanwhile, back at the INS office, no one had heard from the editor, and his column was needed for the next edition. Finally, somebody in authority turned to Charlie and said, "You know how the guy writes. Do a column yourself on anything at all that has to do with baseball and sign his name and get it along to the press-room."

So Charlie did bat out a column-length piece that had nothing whatsoever to do with the Cubs and didn't think about it again until the following day, when the editor returned to the office. He motioned to Charlie to come into a private corner and lectured him.

"Einstein, I don't know how they reached you in whatever bar you were in when I phoned you yesterday. You must have been drunker than a skunk. Everything you managed to write was pure gibberish. Watch your step, kid. I'll cover for you this time, but it better not happen again!"

The story Charlie told me about Willie Mays took place in 1965, when Willie was a star for the San Francisco Giants. One of his teammates was Warren Spahn, who was much older and was more or less sitting out the end of his notable career with that club. Fourteen years earlier, in 1951, Mays had been a rookie on the New York Giants and had hit the first home run of his major league career off Spahn, then ace pitcher for the Boston Braves. Now, in 1965, Mays stepped up to the plate and connected for the 500th home run of his career. It was a highly emotional moment, with the fans standing and roaring their applause as Willie circled the

bases, tipped his cap, and flopped down on the bench in the Giants'
dugout next to his old pal and confidant, Warren Spahn. Spahn put
his arm around Willie's shoulders and hugged him.

"Tell me, Willie," he asked, "did you have the same feeling as
you had back when you hit number-one off me?"

"Yup," was the answer, followed by a pause. "Same sucker
pitch served up to me, too," he added.

Ed Linn has explained to me that when both the subject and the
ghostwriter of an "as-told-to" story take a book seriously (which is
often not the case, because a book doesn't loom particularly large
to some celebrities), a good ghost gains an added dimension to his
normal writing. He becomes like an actor portraying a role, trying
to put himself in the other person's mind as far as language and
frame of reference are concerned. If the ghost can pull it off, the
line between subject and writer is so blurred by the time the book
is done that it no longer really separates the two.

Ed Linn is indeed a notable example of first-class ghostwriting.
He did it both in his books with Bill Veeck and in his collaboration
with Leo Durocher. I regret that I was the editor-publisher of only
the last of these, Durocher's *Nice Guys Finish Last;* Linn's *Veeck as
in Wreck* was published previously by Putnam's. It is just about as
brilliant a book of that genre as will ever be written, and I would
love to have had a hand in it. Well, at least it put me onto how good
Linn was and spurred me to snap up the Durocher project when it
was offered to me. That turned out to be a mighty good book, too,
for Leo had an extraordinary baseball career. He not only played on
the picturesque St. Louis Gas House Gang team but also subsequently became manager, first of the Brooklyn Dodgers, and then
of their hated rivals, the New York Giants.

Durocher talked very freely with Linn when he was being
interviewed and sometimes would tell him things of a particularly
sensitive nature, because he and Ed had an understanding that
Durocher could decide whether to use it or not when he saw how it

looked in manuscript. One of the people he discussed in greatest depth was his particular pal, Frank Sinatra, who had also promised to write an introduction for the book. Neither Linn nor I had ever seen Sinatra, who was very busy at the beginning of his comeback tour after a brief but well-publicized retirement, but we'd been hearing about him constantly from Leo. The book was all ready to go, but we were waiting for the long-promised introduction. We had even pushed back the date for going to press, although we were supposed to be on a crash schedule. Sinatra seemed to be very serious about his introduction. Leo reported that he wanted to read the first part of the manuscript before writing it, so that he would have an idea of the tone and style of the book—not because he wanted to use the same style but because he didn't want his contribution to clash with the general tone. "Contrapuntal" was how he described what he wanted to do. Pretty impressive buildup, and we all were waiting with bated breath for the introduction to come in—but it didn't.

Then one day—nearly the last moment that we could wait—Durocher made a date to come to my office. Linn was to be there, too, and we both expected that at last we'd get the Sinatra introduction. It may even have been promised, but although Leo did pull out some four pages of "Sinatra stuff" as soon as he settled down, it wasn't the introduction. It was a new batch of material about Sinatra. Only God and Leo knew who had written it, and the idea was to insert it in place of a long and colorful section that had emerged out of Linn's interview sessions with Durocher a long time before.

The original text contained some first-rate, mildly rowdy stories stemming from a tour of the Pacific on which Leo had accompanied Frank. One had to do with Sinatra taking on some Australian photographers who had literally forced his car off the highway at top speed in order to get some pictures of him. Another told of how he belted a robber he caught in his hotel suite. Others were about several macho practical jokes that Sinatra had played on Durocher, on the ballfield and off, often hilarious but also largely of a hooligan nature. That kind of stuff was good for the book: it came as a change of pace and also could be used, in the initial promotion, to indicate that there was more in the book than who had won a game on a certain Wednesday in Cincinnati.

Now to be inserted in its place were these four new pages that Leo had produced like a magician pulling a rabbit out of a top hat, and it amounted to nothing but an extended paean by Durocher to Sinatra. One line went: "Looking back over our years together, I'd say Frank has been as good to me as he's been to humanity. Which means he's my best friend, too."

Well, the book wasn't going to rise or fall on what Leo had to say about Frank Sinatra, and any real disappointment I felt was because we had run out of time and wouldn't be getting an introduction from Sinatra, which would have been helpful. But I looked over at Ed Linn as he finished reading it, and I could see the blood drain from his face.

"Leo," he said, "this stuff reads like a eulogy. And do you know what the worst part of it is? If this goes in the book, you'll be doing Sinatra, as well as yourself, a disservice. It will look as if you have to kiss his ass in order to be his friend."

Durocher had a colorful expression for describing a man who had reached the upper limits of anger. Writing about how Jackie Robinson would react after he had been knocked down by a pitch, Durocher said, "Jackie bounced up so mad that he swelled up like a porpoise. He looked like he was going to explode." Well, I'll be damned if Leo's face didn't turn blood red and seem to swell up to nearly twice its size as he heard Linn's pronouncement. "This is my book!" he shouted, looking as if he was about to explode, "and it's going to read the way I want it."

Ed suggested that Leo at least show the stuff that had been taken out to Sinatra, and ask him if he found anything there objectionable, because by this time it had become clear that Durocher had thought better of the rowdy stories, had never shown them to

Sinatra, and had simply substituted this pap. Almost immediately it became equally clear that there was little chance that Leo was going to follow Ed's suggestion.

The atmosphere was extremely steamy, and Linn's face had changed from red to ashen pale and sweaty. Durocher looked like Dizzy Gillespie hitting a high note. I walked behind Durocher's chair and signaled to Ed to drop it. Somehow, without clearing matters up at all, we dropped the subject. The mood turned pleasant again, and when Durocher and Linn left my office together, they were the best of buddies once more.

But about an hour later my telephone rang, and it was Ed Linn on the line calling from his home. Pretty soon I got the picture. Ed had interpreted my signal to him to mean that of course I agreed with him, and just leave it to good old Peter to bring Durocher around to our way of thinking in the end.

Of course I did agree with him, but he couldn't have been more wrong about why I signaled him. I meant him to knock it off because he, not Durocher, was out of line. "It *is* Durocher's book", I told him. "It's the autobiography of Leo Durocher. When a person writes his autobiography, he, not the writer, is responsible for everything in it, and he is therefore entitled to put in, or take out, anything he wants to."

There was a long pause, and I could only hope I hadn't sent Ed back into another sweatbox. At last he said, "You're right, and I certainly should know it. When I was working with Bill Veeck on his book, and we were going over the final manuscript, Bill decided that he had given Rogers Hornsby a worse pummeling than an old guy long out of baseball deserved or was worth. I vehemently accused Bill of running scared, and he informed me that it didn't matter what I thought. He said, 'It's my book, and those two pages are out.'

"He was, of course, right, and in trying to explain my temper tantrum before I left the next day, I said, 'You have to understand, Bill, that by this time I think I made you up.'

" 'Don't worry about it,' Veeck said. 'You have to understand that by this time I think I wrote the book.'

"It was the perfect response, and I would have thought it had taught me a lesson that would stick with me forever. But somehow I seem to have forgotten it today. It's Durocher's book, all right. Sorry I bothered you."

There is a postscript to this saga. The Sinatra introduction came in too late to make the book itself, so we extracted a brief portion and put it in a box on the flap of the jacket. That brought a letter from Sinatra's lawyer, saying we could use all of it or none of it. We informed the lawyer that we were taking it out on the next batch of jackets.

CHAPTER 2

The Splendid Splinter

Inside Ted Williams

There are star ghosts and there are mundane ones, those who are assigned a job merely because they're known to be professionally competent in a certain field. They're not expected to do much more than pursue their homework with respect to what has already been written about the athlete whose book they're to write, have an interview or two with him or her, grind out anything from an acceptable to an admirable manuscript, and go back to their regular line of writing again. They may never give the book they ghosted another thought, except to hope it will produce further earnings for them over and above their guaranteed base fee. I don't say that most ghostwriters are as cold-blooded as that, for they aren't, but I do claim that it is the rare collaborator on a sports book who carries matters past the completion of the job at hand. Usually there's no practical reason why he should. Sometimes, however, an athlete has a complex and intriguing personality that captures a sensitive collaborator's imagination enough so that he wants to build a lasting relationship.

One such case involved baseball's immortal star, Ted Williams, and the writer who ghosted three books with him, John Underwood. I published all three of those books, two on baseball and one on fishing, Williams's other passion. While I never really had the opportunity to get to know Williams, I think I now understand the

11

sort of man he is better than I do most of the other athletes I
worked with on a more personal basis. You see, Underwood continues to be a friend of mine, and in the intervening years John and
Ted, who both live in the Miami area, have become close fishing
and hunting companions. From the beginning, Underwood has
been fascinated by the inner man behind the great batting star's
well-known exterior. Recently Underwood has told me stories that
offered me an unusual insight into aspects of Williams that I, a
knowledgeable sports fan, never knew before, although he was an
idol of mine, particularly back in 1941.

Any real baseball buff will know why Williams was an idol for
many, so I'll just set the facts down here briefly for the benefit of
readers who are only moderately familiar with baseball history and
statistics and who have never read Williams's autobiography, *My
Turn at Bat,* published in 1969. But first, let me tell an anecdote
that conveys the integrity and spirit that Williams brought to
baseball. In 1941, when his team, the Boston Red Sox, was going
to Philadelphia to play out the final two games of the season,
Williams was batting .3996, which rounds out to .400. That is an
incredibly wonderful batting average for a season, and achieving it
gives a batter an assured place in baseball's Hall of Fame. In this
century only seven men had previously done it, and they were
acknowledged immortals like Ty Cobb, George Sisler, and Rogers
Hornsby. (Babe Ruth never did it, nor did Joe DiMaggio, nor, for
that matter, has anyone else in the close to half a century since
1941.)

The two games that were to close out the season were to be
played as a double-header and were meaningless as far as the
pennant race was concerned: both Boston and Philadelphia were
out of it. So the Boston manager told Williams that it would be
perfectly all right for him to sit on the bench that day and not play
at all, if he chose to do so. That would assure the preservation of
his precious .400 average as the batting champion for that year. But
Williams, competitive sportsman that he was, wouldn't have it that
way. He played *both* games and made six hits: 4 for 5 times at bat in

the first game, and 2 for 3 in the second! And what did that make his final 1941 batting average? .406!

After winning the batting championship again the following year, Williams went off to fight in World War II, sacrificing four of what would surely have been peak years of his baseball career. But after the war he was still the old Ted, leading the league again in 1947 and 1948. Called into the service again for the Korean war, he came back once more to win his fifth batting championship in 1957 (when he batted an amazing .388) and his sixth in 1958. Many are convinced he was the greatest hitter of all time, with due respect to other possible claimants like Ty Cobb, Rogers Hornsby, and Babe Ruth. In addition to being such a great batter, he made an intense study of the art, and his book *The Science of Hitting*, published in 1972, which is one of the three books on which John Underwood was his collaborator and I the publisher, is the acknowledged classic on the subject.

The third book the pair wrote together wasn't published until 1982, and is about the other sport in which Williams has become almost as famous as in baseball, big-game fishing. I am pretty sure that working together on *Fishing the Big Three,* sharing fishing experiences over the years with an intimacy that couldn't have been possible in writing the baseball books, made the two men lifelong friends. In the course of editing all three of the Williams-Underwood books, my own contacts with Ted were no more than peripheral. Underwood was the person I worked with for the most part, for he was on hand in New York and the manuscripts I was waiting for came from his typewriter. Without John's filling me in, from my own limited experience I could never have delved into the secret sort of person Williams is. It became more and more fascinating as Underwood talked to me in the course of being interviewed for this book.

In 1969, when Williams had a new job managing the Washington Senators and Underwood was a staff feature writer for *Sports Illustrated,* the magazine gave John the assignment to fly to Africa, where Williams was on safari prior to the new season.

Underwood was to come back with a long, introspective story about Williams and the ideas and techniques he had used in winning the Manager of the Year award the previous season. John figured he could do the necessary interviewing in a very few days' time, considering how well he already knew Ted, but as he neared the very end of the time he had allotted, he found that he'd been completely unable to pin Williams down to talking about the subject. When they had talked at all about baseball, the conversation would invariably be taken over by Williams's obsession concerning the one and only way to swing a bat, and that's not what *Sports Illustrated* was interested in at that moment. The magazine had run reams of material about Williams as a batter, including the entire text and illustrations of *The Science of Hitting,* but now they were purely interested in his thoughts about his new career—managing a big-league team. Finally John exploded.

"Damn it, Ted," he expostulated one day, "I've a deadline to meet with *Sports Illustrated,* and even if I had all the material right now, I'd barely have time to write my story and get it in so that it can make the issue of *S.I.* that will come out the week the baseball season opens. So far you haven't given me a single new thing to write about, no matter how hard I've tried to lead you around the subject. I've simply got to catch a plane back to New York tomorrow night if I'm going to make it. How about forgetting the safari, or general baseball talk about hitting, or gin rummy, and settling down with me for a solid day's work talking about managing the Senators?"

Williams grinned.

"Look, John, I knew you were coming and for what purpose, and I thought out, and even wrote down, everything I wanted to say that you'll need. But I've been stalling you on purpose. I didn't want you to get your stuff and take off because you're better company than what else is around. But if you're *really* on the spot and have to go tomorrow, I guess I've had my fun. Let's start right now—we won't need anything like a full day. I've got it all so well in mind that it shouldn't take more than a couple of hours."

It didn't, Underwood assured me, and then he went on.

"Ted is the most ambivalent personality you're ever likely to meet. You remember how arrogant he always seemed to be to his own Boston Red Sox fans and sportswriters, refusing to tip his cap when applauded riotously and even spitting on occasion to show his disgust. But that's because he felt they were his equals and in a position to take the heat. He can ridicule or nag long-standing friends, even when they're dear to him, and he overreacts if somebody, even a bosom pal, fails to carry out a commission. But the fact that he can fly off the handle with his peers is balanced by two things. In anything important he's intensely loyal, and he also is incredibly patient and hospitable with people he feels have had less advantages than he. His charity in a monetary sense is well known. Less so is the gentle and welcoming way he will treat a down-and-outer or, for that matter, a well-meaning fool. It is probably an inheritance handed down to him from his mother, who was a fanatical worker for the Salvation Army and was almost obsessed with carrying out its good works.

"The two sides of Ted make him an enigma to some people. On the one hand I know that no one is more desirous of company— often at times when you wouldn't expect him to be—but on the other, his frequent negativism about individuals is likely to make one think that he really doesn't like people. He does. He just picks his spots more carefully than most of us.

"Ted doesn't mind spending money for things he really wants, like fishing equipment or a boat. But he's a frugal man about most personal possessions, and his clothes in particular. He shops for bargains and is most likely to outfit himself completely at the local Army and Navy surplus store. But let any big bill come along, from a meal with people in a fine restaurant to traveling with a friend to Arkansas to hunt or to the Maine coast to fish, and I never saw Ted fail to pick up the check. He comes so close to getting insulted if anyone else tries to pay, that eventually it becomes hard to keep a fifty-fifty relationship with him, and not feel indebted to him.

"But let's get back to the topic about which he is the acknowledged greatest authority—hitting a baseball. One time we were in a small boat together, fishing off the Florida Keys, and Ted decided that was the appropriate time and place to explain lucidly to me his two key batting principles. The first is that the batter's hips have to pivot forward into the swing well before the hands ever do; the second is that the swing through the ball should invariably be on a slightly upward plane. He stood up unexpectedly and demonstrated so violently that, although he didn't quite upset the boat, a lot of nice gear that we both would much rather not have lost went overboard and sank forever.

"One of the most impressive things I ever saw Ted do took place only about half a dozen years ago, along about 1980, when Ted was more than sixty years old and hadn't swung a bat in earnest for more than a decade. Ted was a good friend of a man named Ron Fraser, who coached the University of Miami baseball team that won the NCAA title. Fraser asked Williams if he'd come and throw out the traditional first ball for the championship game, the way celebrities do on important baseball occasions like Opening Day or the first game of the World Series.

"Ted agreed—there would be nothing to it except to lob a ball to the Miami catcher, smile for the photographers, and then go back and sit in the stands. But when he got to the park he learned that Fraser had come up with another, much more ambitious wrinkle. Instead of throwing out the first ball, Ted, known primarily as a batter, should step up to the plate and *hit* the first ball. Fraser, a former minor league pitcher, would feed up five balls and Ted would take a cut at any that he thought he could hit.

"Ted was dressed the way he invariably slouches around Miami, in an old, wildly patterned Honolulu shirt, dungarees, and crepe-soled shoes he had picked up at an Army and Navy store some years before. He didn't look like a fashion plate—much less like a baseball player. He sauntered down onto the field and watched Fraser warming up his arm. 'Can't you throw harder than that, Ron?' he inquired. 'Those pitches are so soft that I won't be able to get any distance when I hit them.'

"Fraser took the chafing in good spirits, but he had his own pride and he did start to bear down with everything he had. Eventually he waved Williams to the plate. He grooved the first pitch, and Williams, a left-handed slugger who invariably hit to right field in his heyday, laid on into the ball and drove it on a screaming line between right and center field, so hard that it rolled right to the fence. Fraser served up another fastball, and Ted did exactly the same thing to that one. And to a third, a fourth, and a fifth pitch. Each hit was almost a mirror image of the preceding one, and every one would have been at least a double in any major league ballpark.

"Fraser took off his cap and made a little bow. 'Want some more, Ted?' he asked. Williams flicked a casual return salute and answered, 'No, thanks, I raised a blister on the fourth ball and tore it open on the fifth. That's enough.' "

CHAPTER 3

Swabbing the Deck in Nancy's Navy

Life with Nancy Lopez. Also with Tommy Armour and Big Bill Tilden

Most sports books are either autobiographies or instruction books "by" a famous athlete and "as told to" or "with" a professional writer, the ghost. Such books may lack the distinction of books of original writing by unusually talented sports authors such as Robert Creamer, who wrote *Babe* and *Casey,* Frank Deford, who wrote *Big Bill Tilden,* or Herbert Warren Wind and Roger Angell, each of whom published several books with my firm of Simon & Schuster. Understandably, that sort of work is a better bet to receive major reviews or be nominated for a book award. But a collaboration between a sports celebrity who really has something to say and a writer who can tune in to the celebrity's wavelength can result in first-rate books. Among those with which I was involved and recall with particular pleasure, apart from those already mentioned, are Rod Laver's book with Bud Collins, Jack Nicklaus's several books with Ken Bowden, Chris Evert's book with Neil Amdur, and Rocky Graziano's *Somebody Up There Likes Me* with Rowland Barber, one of the best boxing books ever written.

On one occasion I unexpectedly turned ghostwriter myself. It was in 1978, when Nancy Lopez, in her rookie year on the Ladies Professional Golf Association tour, became the athletic sensation of the year, accomplishing the incredible feat of winning five tournaments *in a row* (in the course of winning 10 during the year). Suddenly she became a national celebrity, her picture gracing the covers not only of the golf magazines and of *Sports Illustrated,* which might be expected, but also of *The New York Times Magazine,* which was really exceptional for a sports figure. She received tremendous coverage and publicity, reaching from national publications like *Time* and *Newsweek* right down the line to modest small-town papers. She made so many appearances on major television shows that one almost could not turn on the set without seeing her. She was dubbed "the wonder woman," and most members of the adoring galleries that followed her in tournaments wore NANCY'S NAVY buttons, a takeoff on the ARNIE'S ARMY buttons worn a few years before by Arnold Palmer fanatics. At the peak of all the hullabaloo about her, I, along with other publishers, went hotfooting it to her agent's office to see if I could secure a Nancy Lopez book for the Simon & Schuster list.

Knowing that I was sure to be up against stiff competition, I had thought out an approach that I felt might be original enough to be enticing to Nancy and her agent. When I sat down with them, I made the following proposal:

"Getting the best publisher or the biggest cash advance shouldn't be your immediate problem here. I think we're the best, particularly on golf books, but all the other major publishers who'll be talking to you are likely to offer more or less the same sort of contract as we're willing to make. But once you say yes to any of us, what are you going to write? Nancy, you are one of the most attractive, warm, idolized persons in the country at this minute, but I doubt whether at the age of twenty-one you have the material in your background to flesh out a good, full-length book. Your childhood and family, yes, and this remarkable year on the golf tour, but that's no more than a long magazine article such as those that have already appeared, duplicating each other to a large extent, in several news-stand publications. You need a real peg to hang a book-length story on, and I believe I may have thought of one.

"You dropped out of college to become a golf professional and you are still learning. I'd suggest that you do a book entitled *The Education of a Woman Golfer,* with chapter titles telling your story in terms of studies and courses that a fuller exposure to an academic education might have given you. Take your childhood and your family's difficult life as not very well-to-do Mexican-Americans in an Anglo community: that could be the subject of the first chapter, 'My Education in Economics and Sociology.' Or, in comparing men's with women's golf, you might have a chapter called 'My Education in Biology.' 'My Education in Psychology' could be about how to play various rivals head to head, and the mental attitude needed in a medal event to hold a lead over the final holes, or to overtake someone who's ahead of you. When you get to the indispensable chapter in which you analyze that unusual swing of yours—obviously, you wouldn't want to leave that out—it could be called 'My Education in Dynamics.'

"Here," I said, pulling a slip of paper out of my pocket that I had prepared beforehand, "are a few more ideas along that general line. Winning so much prize money plus earning a lot more for product endorsements, you must have enough material for an interesting chapter on 'My Education in Business Administration,' I should think. And there are an awful lot of numbers in golf that could more than justify a chapter called 'My Education in Mathematics': there's scoring in medal play, and the yardage that distinguishes the various pars on each hole adding up to the lengths of different courses, and then of course there is the designation of the different clubs by numbers. Then, golf being the sort of up-and-down game it is, even if you're the best player in the world, you win some and you lose some as well. That might make for a very interesting chapter on 'My Education in Philosophy,' don't you think? And finally, you always give a lot of credit to your caddie, Roscoe Jones, for your success, and seem to be very simpatica with him, to say nothing of the fact that you're in love and are going to get married! What about 'My Education in Chemistry'?"

Having made my pitch, I went back to my office; I had barely arrived when the telephone rang. Nancy was at the other end, and she said, "My agent tells me you're a writer as well as an editor. Would *you* write that book with me?"

What a question! How could I possibly think of declining? Sure I would! Not only would my firm, Simon & Schuster, get this most desirable book, but I'd have a writing assignment that promised to be profitable and great fun, and an intriguing challenge as well. I would have to adapt my way of thinking and expressing myself to her ideas and her youthful vernacular, for this would be an auto-biography, told in the first person by Nancy herself. I would have to turn myself, a man in his sixties, into a 21-year-old young woman! I did pull it off—how successfully is not for me to say—but Nancy seemed to like it, and the book fared well enough, even if no one got immensely rich on it. It was my one and only experience as a ghostwriter, and I enjoyed it thoroughly. It gave me a new perspective on the challenges a ghostwriter faces.

Among all the sports books I handled for my firm I can think of only two athletes who really wrote their own books without profes-sional help from a ghostwriter, and even one of them, Tommy Armour, wasn't completely on his own. Armour was a great golfer in the late twenties and early thirties whose name ranks with those of Bobby Jones, Walter Hagen, and Gene Sarazen as one of the four golfing immortals of the Golden Age of Sport. But despite his record as a player, which includes winning both the United States Open and the British Open, Armour's fame rests even more solidly on his achievements of a quarter of a century or so later, when he became the outstanding teaching professional in the world. At his post at the Boca Raton Club in Florida, Armour taught duffers how to lower their scores by an incredible number of strokes. And whenever champion tournament players of that day, men or women, found their games going a bit sour, they made a beeline for Boca Raton to get a few analytical sessions with the master. For a long time Armour resisted the blandishments of book publishers who wanted him to write an instruction book, but I finally was able to persuade him, and the result was one of the happiest experiences I ever enjoyed as a publisher. Tommy's book, *How to Play Your Best Golf All the Time,* turned out to be what is generally considered the classic golf instruction book of all time, and it has certainly been the best-selling one. In its original year of publication, 1953, it became the number-one best-selling nonfiction book in the country for some weeks on the *New York Times*'s best-seller list, which is incredible for a sports instruction book. It sold hundreds of thousands of copies in hardcover before it appeared in paperback. These remain in print and sell steadily in the thousands even now, more than 30 years after the book was published, and without a line of promotion or advertising for decades.

Tommy was an educated man and a highly talented one in several fields. He excelled in all sports and games, including not only contract bridge and gin rummy, at both of which he could have made a living had it ever been necessary, but also chess. Tommy was completely capable of writing his book without any help, and I know that essentially he did, for I saw the original longhand manuscript. But after that stage he turned it over to his pal of many years, Herb Graffis, one of the deans of golf writers, essentially to get it typed and to produce a clean manuscript that could be sent to me at Simon & Schuster. There's little doubt that Herb copyedited while typing, and he also may have contributed some of his expertise to putting the manuscript into shape, but neither Tommy, the most generous of men, nor Herb ever thought of Herb's work as constituting ghostwriting, and there never was any mention of Graffis's receiving joint credit for authorship of the book. Herb even gracefully declined to have his name mentioned in the author's acknowledgment. His feeling was that Armour was known as a big brain in the golfing community, and he didn't want that image to be tarnished even the tiniest bit by the implication that Armour needed a collaborator.

Our publishing house had no relationship, contractual or otherwise, with Graffis, and I knew nothing of his connection with the Armour book until the finished publication actually existed. Only some time later did I learn from Herb that Tommy split all his earnings from the book right down the middle with him, a fantastically generous private arrangement, but typical of the sort of gesture this fine man was capable of making. Graffis had been going through some fairly rough financial times, and the huge success of the Armour book made him a comfortably rich man. Every Christmas for many years I received a card regularly from Herb in Florida, and each time under the address at the top he penned, "From the house that Tommy and Peter built."

The other sports author I published was Big Bill Tilden, who didn't use a ghost at all—not even a minor helping hand such as Graffis supplied to Armour. Tilden wrote his book *How to Play Better Tennis* when he was nearing 60 years of age and serving a term on a prison farm in California on a charge of homosexually molesting a minor. One day I happened to be in Richard Simon's office when a battered envelope addressed to Simon, the president of the firm, arrived in the mail. It contained a manuscript written in pencil on sheets torn from a long, lined yellow pad. The manuscript came from Tilden, then universally acknowledged as the greatest tennis player who ever lived—he is still so regarded by a great many—and had been marked acceptable for mailing by the prison farm censor.

Dick Simon had published Tilden's first book, *The Common Sense of Tennis*, more than a quarter of a century before, in 1924, as part of Simon & Schuster's very first list. That was during the era when Tilden dominated the tennis world as champion, and securing him for his fledgling firm's first list had been an exciting publishing coup for Dick, a keen tennis player himself. Now, Dick was the boss of an established and much bigger outfit, and he had learned to delegate. I was a fairly new employee then, more involved with business matters than anything else. But Dick knew that I was good enough at tennis to beat him, and he appointed me the resident tennis guru on the spot and turned over the manuscript to me for consideration. Thus I became Tilden's editor and had my appetite whetted to become an editor and go after other sports books as a fun part of the job. I continued to do so for the next three decades.

After Tilden served his term and was released, he came east for what turned out to be the last time. In the course of making arrangements about his book's publication, we planned a tennis match in which I and a good young professional played against Tilden and a friend of mine who was in my playing class. I soon found that what had been said about Tilden just a few years before, when he was past his mid-fifties, had very probably been true. It was said that he was still the best player in the world—for one set, before he tired. He had beaten Bobby Riggs, then the world's top professional, in the first set of a match, and he had also taken the first two sets from Wayne Sabin, also a world-class professional, before running out of steam and eventually losing. He still was immensely impressive in our friendly little doubles match, obviously restraining his game most of the time so as not to overwhelm us and ruin our fun, but doing whatever was necessary to keep us in our place at critical moments. He didn't want to lose, and he didn't.

We talked quite a lot about the theories and tactics he spelled out in his book, and it was clear from the beginning that Bill didn't need a ghostwriter or collaborator and also didn't take too kindly to an editor's queries or suggestions. Tilden was sure he knew everything there was to know about tennis, and he probably was right, so I can't claim I contributed much to this book apart from finding a good artist to illustrate the points Tilden made about strokes. I did, however, get a chance to pour out to him my own tennis concern of the moment after a session in 1950 when we went over the manuscript in galley form just before sending it to press.

I had just staggered through a semifinal match in the singles championship tournament in the Connecticut town where we always spent the summer. I had just barely beaten a player to whom I had never lost a set before and whom I had often beaten handily, and my weakness had been caused by a simple case of nerves at critical times when I was serving late in a set. The thought of getting into the finals and possibly winning this boondocks title had been so awesome and overpowering that each time I tossed a ball up for a serve, it invariably went off anywhere except where I intended to place it—directly overhead. It was the only time in a long tennis career when I absolutely could not control the toss regularly. Without any consistency the ball wandered too far right, or left, or forward, or back, or high, or low. Finally, in desperation, I was simply poking at the ball wherever it happened to be on a particular toss and wafting a series of gentle, sitting-duck serves that gave my opponent every chance to become the aggressor, despite the fact that I was serving. Luckily, no other part of my game was affected by this neurosis, and I was enough better than he to be able to pull out the match successfully. But the experience had been very upsetting, and after all, I still had the finals to play next weekend. Did Tilden have any thoughts or advice about the matter?

He certainly did. He gave me a tip that I had never heard before and have never encountered since from anyone else. He hadn't thought it was important enough to include in his book, and trying to squeeze it in now, at that late stage of production, would have been very difficult. So to the best of my knowledge the piece of instruction that you will encounter as the leadoff in the following chapter has never appeared in print before. For that matter, neither have any of the other sports tips you'll find there.

CHAPTER 4

A Scattering of Sports Tips

On tennis, golf, football, baseball,
track, and poker

Tilden never wrote about this particular aberration in the copious tennis writings he authored. I am recalling as accurately as I can what he told me in person, hence the quotation marks.

A Tennis Tip from Bill Tilden

"Having a normally accurate service toss unaccountably go haywire happens to a lot of players, even pretty good ones. Usually, as is obvious in your case, it's pressure and nerves that causes it. Here's what you might try if it happens to you again. Instead of holding the ball palm up and fingers outstretched in a gracious curl (as if helping your grandmother alight from a car), turn your hand over and inward toward your body until the curve formed by your forefinger and thumb is on top and you can nestle the ball snugly there, the way you'd hold an ice-cream cone. Now your normal upward arm will deliver the ball straight up to where you want to place it, because there won't be any finger-flick action. That's the thing that usually makes for the sort of erratic tosses you describe."

Tilden was absolutely right, and to this day, 35 years later, I still

26

resort to his technique whenever I'm having serious trouble with my toss. I'm not quite sure why I don't use it regularly. It's probably because I never heard of anyone else who did so, and I'm too much of a comformist. In any event, my confidence having been restored by knowledge of this crutch, I did win the final match the next weekend and thus gratify my overweening aspiration to reign over the tennis empire of a small Connecticut village. And they say that Caesar was ambitious!

A GOLD TIP FROM TOMMY ARMOUR

Tommy was a great personal friend of mine. In fact, he was a godfather to one of my children. But I never felt that it would be right for me to ask him to see if he could do anything about my execrable golf game. For one thing, I really didn't care that much, not being a real golfer and only playing very occasionally at a publishers' convention or some such event. For another, I knew that although Tommy got a king's ransom for giving even one lesson on a lesson tee, our relationship was such that he would be adamant about not charging me—even if I were willing to pay a king's ransom for a golf lesson. Consequently, I never brought up the subject, though I visited him in golf settings several times.

Yet there came a day when I broke my rule. Tommy came to my office after we'd had a long, chummy lunch together, and, mellowed by that, plus perhaps a little stimulation from the liquid refreshment that accompanied it, I said, "Tommy, we're having our sales conference down in Dorado Beach next week, and there'll be golf on the program. Mostly I intend to play tennis, but once or twice a year, at times like this, I like to try my hand at a round of golf. But I'm embarrassed.

"I know I'm strong enough to hit a fairly long ball, if only now and then, but I never *do*. In tennis I can hit hard drives off both my forehand and backhand and can get in an untouchable service ace every so often. I bowl a decent ball, too, so it isn't a matter of strength. I'm not too terribly awful at the short game, but I simply cannot connect for any distance off the tee, or with a fairway wood or a long iron. At best I get a lazy, high shot, usually with a slice, that has no *whack!* and travels no farther than half or two-thirds of the distance such a shot should carry. Yet I know all the theories in golf books, including your own, about getting distance: the pivot, the long, full backswing, the action of the hips and knees, cocking the wrists and holding in the hitting area until unleashing just before contact, and the full follow-through. Words, Tommy, all words in books that I've even edited, but as far as I'm concerned, words that don't work."

Tommy asked me if I had a cane or an umbrella in my closet. Yes, there was an umbrella, and Tommy said in his soft Scottish burr that he'd like to see me take a full golf swing with it. (My office was big enough back then so that this was not at all dangerous.) I swung a couple of times, and he said, "Not so bad, but now let's see something else. Use the umbrella as a tennis racquet this time, and show me your forehand drive." I did so, and he said, "Ah! Do it again, but very, very slowly." As I took up position, but before I ever started the stroke, Tommy said, "Look at your hand and see how loosely your fingers are gripping the umbrella." I could see that my grip was extremely loose, with no pressure being applied at all. "Now take your swing—slowly," Tommy ordered, and he called, "Stop!" just as I was about to contact the imaginary ball. "Look at your grip now," he said, and it was immediately clear what he was getting at. My fingers had firmed up and my grip was about as tight as it could be.

"M'boy," said Tommy, "when you took those golf swings you didn't look so great, but not so bad either. I've seen plenty worse who could hit a ball a long way when they connected. But at the top of your backswing you were hanging onto that grip so tightly that it would have taken a team of horses to pry it loose. Sure, you cocked your wrists at the top and didn't turn them loose on the downswing until when you're supposed to, *but nothing changed in your fingers all the way.* You were hanging on like grim death from top to bottom. You didn't do that on your tennis stroke and I know you wouldn't if you were throwing a ball. On all those motions a person starts with a very loose grip and then tightens up on it just before the moment of truth. Try that next week on the golf course."

I did try it and did indeed hit a number of balls 50 to 100 yards farther than I ever had before. Not all of them, of course, but when I managed to connect with the ball, the shots went booming away with a crispness I'd never enjoyed off the tee or the fairway in the past. I had received a fabulously good tip in my office from Tommy. It's irrelevant that I didn't score any better than usual, because my short game went all to pieces. It has been truly written that golf is a humbling game.

A FOOTBALL TIP FROM GEORGE ALLEN

It's hard to explain why George Allen kept being let go as head coach by team after team in the National Football League, for all through those years, in the late 1970's, he was consistently compiling one of the most impressive winning records any coach has ever enjoyed. If you'd like to read his side of the story—and I found him to be a forthright and believable fellow—get yourself a copy of a book he wrote for Simon & Schuster on which I was his editor. It's titled *Merry Christmas, You're Fired!*

At the time we were working together on the book, 1981, George was once again out of a coaching job and instead was being the color commentator on Vin Scully's telecasts of NFL games over the CBS network. A nice job if you can get it: seeing the best athletes play a game you love from a cozy, heated press-box booth weekend after weekend without too much work, no real responsibility, and a pleasant salary. George was quite gung-ho about becoming an author and he pitched into the work with enthusiasm. Being his editor was both amusing and rewarding—especially when he suggested I join him in the booth at Giants Stadium in New Jersey's Meadowlands and see a game from that vantage point.

It was December, and during a quiet interval we started talking about the probable winners and the early betting line on a number of interesting college bowl games that were coming up. George said something like this: "You can pay all your Christmas bills, year after year, by knowing about bowl games and betting the right way. The beautiful part is that you don't have to know a thing. Expertise, judgment, past records, statistics—none of those have to be considered. Simply take the points, and bet on every underdog.

"The reason is simple. Bowl games are arranged to be between teams that should be more or less even rivals, so it's unlikely that the underdog is really outclassed. And the pressure to perform well in a bowl game, with a national TV audience looking on, exists for both teams, but particularly for the favorite. They make errors and they're likely to play cautiously once they get a lead. Nonfavorites actually win just about as much as favorites, and when you're betting on them and being given points, you'll win much more often than you lose. It's one of the best bets in sports."

A little research shows that Allen's Simple System to Get Rich outperforms any financial advice service you're likely to find advertised in the *Wall Street Journal*. Listen to this. There have been an average of about 16 bowl games played each year over the six years since George told me his great secret, through the January 2, 1987 games. In the approximately 100 games played in that six-year period, if you had taken the points and bet on the underdog in each one, you would have won about 50 percent of the time, lost about 40 percent of the time, and broken even on the rest.

That's quite a nice edge to have, but a simpler bet has proved even better. Just confine your operations and bet only on the major bowl games, the five that keep fanatics glued to their TV sets for practically the entire New Year's holiday period—the Rose Bowl, the Sugar Bowl, the Cotton Bowl, the Orange Bowl, and the Fiesta Bowl. In these games the pressure on college-age athletes is particularly intense. The results for six years? In those 30 games you'd have 21 winners and only 9 losers!

You may be gone from the football scene, George, but you'll not be forgotten by anyone who listened to you.

A BASEBALL TIP FROM THE AUTHOR

It's a common experience for many to take someone who knows absolutely nothing about baseball—say a foreigner or quite a small child—to see a game. If you happen to do that, what is the very first thing you should say to try to explain this game, invariably an incomprehensible one to a newcomer?

I can venture a number of replies you might give to that question, and all of them would be sensible, and all of them would be wrong. You might, for example, say:

1. There are four bases, and if a player can make his way around all four, he scores a run, and the team with the most runs wins.
2. A game lasts for nine innings, with each team having a chance to come to bat.
3. The pitcher tries to strike out the batter while the batter is trying to make a hit. Three strikes and the batter is out; four balls where the pitcher doesn't throw the ball over the plate—I'll explain what the plate is later—means that the batter can walk to first base. I guess I'd better start all over again.
4. It's questionable whether it was Abner Doubleday or Alex Cartright who invented baseball, but it's a game that seems to be derived from an English children's game called rounders.
5. A man will come around selling hot dogs any minute now.

That list could go on for a long time, for the nuances of this wonderful but complicated game are hard to grasp unless one simple fact is understood at the very beginning. This fact is not true of other team sports with which the newcomer to baseball might already be familiar. That fact is: *At all times during a baseball game, all of the nine people on one team are trying to stop one person on the other team from doing something.*

That isn't the game of baseball in a nutshell, but it is the shell. Until it's cracked you can't get at the nut.

A TRACK TIP FROM EXPERIENCE

It's a natural inclination, when trying to find the best seat from which to watch a track meet, to select one right on or near the finish line of most of the races, if possible. Sometimes it is a good idea, because the designers of a few arenas and stadiums have actually considered making things good for track spectators. They have planned it so that the people in front of you, or to your left, do not block your view as you're desperately trying to peer to your left to see runners coming down the homestretch. Yet even at the few good sites you're likely to have difficulty getting an unobstructed view because you can be sure that at the critical final stage of a close race some people will stand up to cheer their favorite home, and when *anyone* stands up in such a situation, *everyone* has to stand up in order to have a chance of seeing anything.

My modest suggestion is to secure your seat at the *other* side of the arena or stadium, opposite the finish line. At indoor meets with comparatively limited seating accommodations—and every seat likely to be reserved in advance—you might not be able to pick and choose, but if you can, pick a seat such as I've indicated. You'll be seeing the finish of races while people who were seated right on the finish line will be asking each other, "Who won?"

At an outdoor meet in a big football stadium, the stands on the side of the finish line may be packed, but right across the way there will be only a handful of sophisticated track fans taking their ease and enjoying the best seats in the house. ("Seats" is right, even if you're alone. There aren't enough track fans to come close to filling a huge football stadium, so if you pick the unpopular side you can sprawl out over several seats and have ample room to park your coat or spread out your lunch.) You will see absolutely everything with no one screening out your vision, and if the figures racing down the stretch are somewhat smaller, what does it matter when you see them so much better? They're still a lot larger than any runners you'd see on the largest home television screen.

AN INGENIOUS AND POSSIBLY HANDY POKER TIP

You can't play poker for matchsticks. It has to cost you real money to raise, call, or bluff, or it isn't poker. Many games in which it's customary to play for stakes, like contract bridge and rummy, can be fun and remain the same game even if no money is involved, but playing poker only for chips is not poker. The element of the bluff is removed, and that's integral to the game.

Back in the 1930's, during the depths of the Depression, I was one of a small crowd of young people who enjoyed one another's company and who wanted to set up a weekly poker session. But there was a catch. We had widely varying incomes, with a couple of us quite well-to-do, by the standards of the times, and others just out of school or college and struggling in a first job at Depression-era salaries. Under those circumstances, how could a poker game open to all be any good? The stakes would be uncomfortably high for some, or so low for others as to make the game comparable to playing for matchsticks. A particular young genius in our group came up with an idea, and it actually worked splendidly.

His plan required that one player agree to act as banker for the game. To be the banker calls for a person to have two attributes. He must be flush enough that any sum likely to be won or lost in this particular poker game is not a vital amount of money to him, and he must be a sport who likes to gamble on affairs that not only offer a good chance to win as well as to lose, but also, regardless of results, will be fun. A good example of such a person would be an angel for a Broadway show. If the show is a hit he may make a fortune, but even if it's a flop he'll meet a lot of interesting people along the way, including the chorus line, if it's a musical.

The banker in our poker game got the same enjoyment out of playing his hands as the rest of us, but he had an additional, and often considerably more important, stake in things. How the other players eventually made out could be much more meaningful to him at the time of settlement than how he fared himself. His own success, or lack of it, affected the results, of course, but he had an all-important side bet going.

This is how it worked. We all were given an identical stack of chips; before the first deal, all the players except the banker wrote on separate slips of paper how much they wanted their piles to represent in money. The clerk or stenographer working at a first job might decide that a $10 stack was quite enough for an initial stake and write down $10. The junior executive might pick $25 or $50, while another friend who'd been out in the business world a few years and had made it to a vice-presidency in his firm might indicate that his stack was worth $100. These slips were folded and, not seen by anyone, were deposited in a drawer. The banker did not write out a slip. His or her result would depend upon how much had to be paid out to the winners, as opposed to how much would be taken in from the losers. Obviously, it was to the banker's advantage to win as many chips as possible, so that no one else could have them, but it was even more vital to the banker that, at the end of the game, he collected more from the losers than he had to pay out to the winners.

This kind of side bet of the banker's was the only aspect of our game making it different from any other poker game. Everyone else could play a regular game. The clerk's chips could raise, or see, the vice-president's chips, even though their actual value was only one-tenth as much. When the vice-president won some of the clerk's chips, they carried his, not the clerk's, valuation. In other words, all the players won or lost at whatever rate their own valuation of their chips dictated. And so the game proceeded to its end normally, with some piles of chips growing, some staying comparatively steady, and some declining and perhaps having to be replenished, in which case a new stack would be supplied, at the same valuation as the original stack.

When it was time to call quits, the banker might have a big pile of chips, or a modest pile, or none. If the banker had won a bundle, the reward was that no payout would be required on those chips, which was plenty of incentive for the banker to play to the limit of his or her ability. For now it was time for accounts to be settled, and the settlement was all in the banker's hands. The drawer containing the slips of paper was opened and the dealer paid out to the winners and collected from the losers on the basis of their own valuations. Obviously, the banker hoped that the ones who had declared low were the winners and the ones who had declared high were the losers, and this was the case just about half the time. For if you think that the big plungers would inevitably be better poker players than the conservative ones, you'd be wrong just about as often as you'd be right. The soundest poker player in our game was the young wife of a man who also played. She was on a household allowance and invariably chose a fairly modest value for her pile. Her husband, a more flamboyant but by no means as good a poker player as she, fixed a much higher value for his pile. The banker usually made out very well in paying out and collecting from this couple.

This unique idea for conducting a competitive and compatible poker game among friends of unequal means may make just as good sense for you today as it did for us in the Depression, for birds of a financial feather don't necessarily flock together all the time, in any era.

CHAPTER 5

Rod Laver and the Fates

My chance for immortality

If Aladdin with his magic lamp had shown up in my office in the spring of 1971 and offered to grant me one wish, he could not have done much better by me than the actual opportunity that came my way just then. I was on the eve of putting out a book by Australia's Rod Laver, a player who at that time dominated the tennis world as few men ever have. His two grand slam years, in which he won all four of the world's major tennis tournaments, were behind him. Now, as a member of a hand-picked field of the world's greatest professional tennis players, he had swept every match in a round-robin tournament involving 16 consecutive head-to-head matches, each for a winner-take-all big-money purse. It was the most spectacular sustained run of wins any tennis player had ever achieved, and that made it the ideal time to publish his autobiography, written with his collaborator "ghost," Bud Collins of the *Boston Globe,* today perhaps better known as the most knowledgeable voice in television tennis coverage. In the course of working on the book, both Laver and Collins had become my good friends.

Although both Rod and Bud knew that I was a fanatically avid tennis player, they also knew that I had no pretentions to being more than a good, club-level performer. One morning I received a phone call from Bud in Boston, suggesting that I travel up to New Hampshire with him to the Mount Washington Hotel in Bretton

Woods to join Rod and his wife, Mary, for the weekend and play a little tennis with them. It was truly as if Bud had materialized in place of Aladdin's jinni. I never agreed to anything faster in my life, and that afternoon I was on my way.

In his television appearance Bud sometimes refers to himself as a "hacker," but he is being extremely modest. He was a very fine amateur player, a good deal better than I, and I was not bad. Mary Laver hit a nice, solid ball, too, but she was clearly the weakest member of the foursome, so it was logical for her to be paired with Rod against Bud and me in our doubles matches. We had some pleasantly close scores, too, as a result, but that was chiefly because Bud and I tried (usually unsuccessfully) to keep the ball away from the far-ranging Rocket Laver. Also, with true Australian gallantry, he restrained himself and played a gracious "customer's game": he hit balls back with real pace but almost never drilled one with the better than 100-mile-per-hour velocity that he'd have used in a genuine competitive match. It was a wonderfully exhilarating and enjoyable experience for me. All of the guests at the huge hotel turned out to see the greatest tennis player in the world in action at close quarters, and I had never played in front of so large and appreciative a crowd.

Realizing beforehand that this would be my chance for immortality, when I had packed in New York I had slipped into my bag our modest home movie camera, hitherto used exclusively to take family films on vacation or at the beach. Now, at the end of one of our sessions of doubles, I somewhat sheepishly pulled it out of my tennis bag and asked Rod if he'd be good enough to rally with me, as if we were playing singles, while Bud or Mary filmed us. "That's a fair dinkum idea, pal," was Rocket's response, and we began.

I created an immediate problem for myself from the outset, as is quite clear to anyone who has ever seen this screen masterpiece. During the actual doubles match, when I had been concentrating upon playing well rather than looking good, I had performed with my usual effective but not particularly formful style. Now, as I heard the whirr of the camera and knew it was focusing on me, I tried to hit my strokes with unaccustomed stylish grace. The results were catastrophic. I erred constantly and generally flubbed my chance to make the film look as if I were actually giving Laver a workout. Near the very end of the short reel, however, I suddenly do look good to the viewer. I had hit one of my best shots, a hard and sharply angled crosscourt forehand drive, deep to the corner, and had rushed to net behind it. Rod is left-handed, so the ball went to his backhand. The bounce took it so far past the sideline that Rod was content merely to block it back, and the ball more or less floated up to me, where I stood poised to put it away at net. Watching the film it does appear that I've finally played a point extremely well, for I follow the flight of the ball intently, left hand raised and fingers pointing at it in the approved textbook style as it descends, go up gracefully off my toes, and smash the ball away to the opposite corner for a sure winner. That's the way it looks on film up to that point, and as I turn and start to walk nonchalantly back toward the baseline, a viewer could well imagine that a small ripple of applause arose from the spectators.

The viewer would not know that I had actually misjudged the ball on the smash and had hit it only with the top of the frame of my racquet, rather than meeting it solidly on the gut. The result had been to send the ball high up in the air behind me. But I knew that my camera was not the greatest mechanism in the world for taking fast action pictures, and I was pretty sure that it wouldn't catch the mishit but would just register the smash and my apparent success at putting the ball away, which is what it did indeed register. That was why, thinking quickly, I assumed the air of nonchalance instead of tearing my hair and cursing. After all, I could hear the camera continuing to take the scene all the while, and I knew there were no time-outs for intermissions.

Well and good. I was pretty sure that I was going to look very good playing against Laver for a few seconds at least. The problem is that as the film continues, a tennis ball suddenly drops out of the heavens right onto the top of my nonchalant head, making obvious to any tennis player what really happened!

The first time my family and I ever ran the film, my younger son, Roger, who is a handy man at such matters, said after the raucous laughter had died down, "Never mind, Dad, I can easily cut that out and splice the film together so it won't appear." I didn't have to ponder over his kind offer very long. I replied, "Thanks, Roger, but in no event is this going to make it as an instruction film. On the other hand, we have here a comedy gag that might well have been in a Marx Brothers or Laurel and Hardy movie. I suggest we let it go at that."

CHAPTER 6

Sorry About That!

Chris Evert meant well

My experience with my favorite male tennis player, Rod Laver, had the somewhat grotesque conclusion just described, but that was peaches and cream compared with my one personal experience involving my favorite woman tennis player, Chris Evert.

Ever since she first appeared on the tennis scene as a teenager in pigtails, Chris has seemed to me to embody everything admirable in a world-famous athlete: ability, modesty, sportsmanship. She still does, and it was with immense pride and satisfaction that I was able to sign her up at the peak of her fame to be one of my authors on the Simon & Schuster list. She was to write her life story, to be entitled *Chrissie,* and her collaborator was to be an old and good friend of mine, Neil Amdur, at that time the tennis expert for the *New York Times,* and today the editor-in-chief of *World Tennis.* As is almost invariably the case when the pages of a book manuscript are being turned out by a collaborator's typewriter, a publisher works with the ghost and may actually never get to see the official author. (That was the case when I published Bjorn Borg's book, *My Life and Game,* when he was at the very top, in 1980. The closest I ever came to Borg was sitting in a front-row box with his ghostwriter, Eugene L. Scott, at the United States Open at Flushing Meadow. Gene brought me back a first copy of the book, with a pleasant inscription to me from Borg, which he had managed to have the star do for me in the dressing room after his match. So I cannot claim that Bjorn and I were ever Damon and Pythias.)

I really have met Chris Evert, however—three times in all. The first was with Neil Amdur when the contract for the book was signed. The second consisted of no more than a handshake and a smile when I was attending another U.S. Open with Steve Flink, also of *World Tennis* and the ultimate authority on tennis history and facts; we ran into Chris on the way to the interview room after a match. Steve is Chris's most devoted fan and a close friend of all the members of her family. As he stopped to say hello and offer congratulations on her win, he said, "You must know Peter, don't you? He's your publisher." She either did remember the one time we had met over the contract or was gracious enough to pretend that she did, but the memory really did carry over to a couple of days later at the same tournament, when I had my third meeting with the lady.

This time I had gone to the interview room myself to listen to her talk. Seeing Neil Amdur sitting up front, I went and took a seat next to him. He was waiting to see Chris about some publicity matter concerning the book. After the crush of admirers and well-wishers had thinned out, he managed to collar her and lead her off to a corner where they could have a cold drink and talk. Neil said they certainly had no secrets to keep from their publisher, so why didn't I come along?

Chris was most affable, too, and was very interested in the fact that the following week I'd be flying down to Florida for the Simon & Schuster sales conference, which was to be held at Boca Raton. My plan was to fly first to Fort Lauderdale to visit my brother, John, who lived there, for a day, and then have him drive me the few miles farther south to Boca Raton.

"Are you planning to play any tennis while you're down there?" asked Chris, who by this time knew I was a keen player who never passed up an opportunity to play.

"Just as much as I possibly can in between the talks I have to give at the sales conference about our forthcoming books, including yours," I told her.

"How about that day in Fort Lauderdale?" she inquired.

I replied that I didn't know anyone in that city except my brother, who wasn't a tennis player at all and probably didn't know any. Chris smiled.

"The biggest tennis establishment in Fort Lauderdale is Holiday Park, which is owned and run by my father, Jimmy. He's not likely to be there when you arrive, but if you just go to the office window and ask for Rose*, who assigns courts and sets up games for people who don't have a partner, and tell her you're my publisher, I promise she'll take care of you."

The idea was irresistible, since I didn't know how much time I'd be able to steal from the sales conference. I had heard about the glories of Jimmy Evert's Holiday Park, and my brother could surely spare me a couple of hours out of the day. The following week I packed all my tennis gear, and very little else, because I knew the conference would be completely informal. I wouldn't even need a jacket or a dress shirt or tie. Slacks and a sports shirt would be an appropriate costume for anything I planned to do. Since I always like to travel light, and the sales conference was only to be for a couple of days, I just packed what I'd be wearing on the plane to Fort Lauderdale, the tennis stuff and one extra sports shirt.

John met my plane in midmorning, and I asked him if he'd mind dropping me at Holiday Park so I could get in a little tennis before joining him for the rest of the day and evening. That was fine with him—actually he had some work he wanted to finish and this would give him a chance. We agreed that I'd simply call for a taxi when my tennis was over.

After he left me at the entrance, I walked up to the office and asked for Rose, who couldn't have been more gracious or helpful when she heard my story. She asked if I wanted to play singles or

---

*Her name probably wasn't Rose. It was long enough ago so that I've forgotten. In any case, I don't claim that what happened was her fault.

doubles, instantly arranged a game for me with players she said would be of my calibre (after I tried to specify what that calibre was), and told me we'd have a court in 15 minutes—just enough time for me to get into tennis togs. She *did* say, very firmly, "Don't leave your valuables in the dressing room. Bring them out onto the court with you."

This made sense, because despite its being as well set up and lovely a tennis complex as anyone would wish to see, it is a public establishment, and most casual people who play there don't have lockers. Fair enough.

There was a long rack with a few hangers. I took off what I was wearing—shirt, slacks, underwear, shoes, and socks—and hung up what was hangable, leaving only my shoes on the floor under my hangers. Dressed in my tennis outfit, I carefully stowed all my valuables in my bag—wallet, wristwatch, keys, coins, and material I needed for the sales conference—and carried the bag out onto the court with my assigned new friends. Rose had arranged a splendid game of doubles, and I enjoyed every minute of the three sets we played. Then I went back to the locker room to take a shower and get dressed.

!!!!!?????!!!!!

The rack was empty! The floor was bare! Not only were my slacks and shirt and shoes gone, but so were my socks and underwear shorts! I was an elderly, perspiring man, dressed in very sweaty tennis clothes, carrying a bag that didn't contain anything fresh to put on except pajamas and a change of tennis clothes. I went back to the office to report to Rose.

She was surprised and shocked and sorry. She reminded me that she *had* warned me to pack up my valuables and not leave them. I agreed that she had indeed, but that this was the first time I had ever thought of my rather modest summer clothes and shoes, to say nothing of my undershorts, as being valuables. Valuable to whom? Certainly not to anyone very fussy, and only to someone of my figure and shoe size. Was that any sort of clue to our tracking down the culprit?

Rose thought not. Neither did I. Luckily, I still had my wallet, so I was able to get a taxi to John's house. Luckily, that wallet contained my credit cards, so I postponed taking a shower at John's until he drove me to a shop where I was able to buy replacements for the missing items. They saw me through that day at Fort Lauderdale and the short stay at Boca Raton, and they're still in what I laughingly refer to as my wardrobe. I wonder if my old stuff has continued to do as well for its new owner. I hope not.

I've never seen Chris Evert again since to talk to, and she doesn't know this story and never will unless she reads this book, or someone who has read it tells it to her. But rest easy, Chris. Rest easy, Rose. Rest easy, Jimmy Evert. I am not litigious. I had a lovely time at Holiday Park on that occasion, and again a couple of years later, when I did not tempt the fates but came to Holiday Park in tennis clothes, and went away in those same tennis clothes. I hold no grudge, but I learned to be careful.

CHAPTER 7

The Golden Bear

Jack Nicklaus sinks a putt

The weekend of the 1986 Masters golf tournament in Augusta, Georgia, saw all the sports-minded members of the family glued to the television set on the final day. They were very much aware of my 25-year involvement with publishing all of Jack Nicklaus books and of my high regard for him. In every sport I have favorite individuals and teams for whom I root, but my desire to see Nicklaus pull off one more miracle in his miraculous career and win a twentieth major championship topped all the rest. Of course, now it was rather unlikely. After all, Jack was 46 years old, and he hadn't won a major title since 1980. Also, he hadn't been playing frequently lately, and when he had played, he'd sometimes done poorly, even failing to make the cut a couple of times. Not like the old Jack.

Admittedly, in this Masters he'd been playing pretty well over the first three days, but as we watched him come to the 10th tee in the fourth and final round, it seemed likely that he might finish in about fifth place at best. Although he was two strokes under par for the tournament at that stage, the great Spanish golfer, Seve Ballesteros, had a lead of some half-dozen strokes lower, and three other world topnotchers, Greg Norman, Tom Kite, and Nick Price, each had a two- or three-stroke lead on him—not to mention Tom Watson, who was virtually barking at his heels. The tournament seemed to be in the bag for Ballesteros, and the best we Nicklaus fans were rooting for was that Jack would hold off Watson and possibly better his position to finish second, third, or fourth.

But then Jack's golf suddenly went crazy, and over those last 10 holes he shot seven under par to win the title and his twentieth major championship by one stroke!

It took quite a while for the excitement in the living room to abate, but when things had quieted down somewhat, one of the youngest members of the clan piped up and asked why Nicklaus's victory seemed to mean so much to me? I never had been so excited or elated over a sports result before. Why Jack Nicklaus in particular?

The fun of having a young child around who, unlike one's older children, has never heard your stories before, is that it reopens an enjoyable world. It makes me truly appreciate a passage from one of my favorite books, written back in 1957, Robert Paul Smith's *"Where did you go?" "Out" "What did you do?" "Nothing,"* published by W. W. Norton:

"My little boy was mooning around the house the other day—it is one of the joys of being a writer that occasionally when I am mooning about the house because I haven't the vaguest idea of what to do about the second act, or the last chapter, or Life, or why I don't have an independent income or a liquor store or a real skill like a tool-and-die maker or a lepidopterist or a mellophone player—I can slope downstairs and trap a child. The little boy was mooning around. I was mooning around. He had no idea what to do with himself because his room is full of wood-burning kits and model ships to be made out of plastic and phonographs and looms and Captain Kangaroo Playtime Kits and giant balloons and plaster of paris and colored pencils and compasses and comic books and money. I will straighten this little bugger out, I said, I will pass on to him the ancient knowledge of his sire . . . by God I will."

Here was my chance, and I made the most of it. I explained that my relationship with Jack Nicklaus dated back to December 1961, when he was still an amateur, before he started to win all those championships as a professional. Mark McCormack, then a young Cleveland lawyer who was handling the business affairs of several top professional golfers, had decided to add Nicklaus to his client list when he turned pro, which was scheduled for the next month. Simon & Schuster had done spectacularly good jobs on golf books in previous years, and the firm had an enviable reputation in that respect, so McCormack came to me first. He told me Nicklaus would be earning considerable money the following year as a professional (I'll bet even he didn't realize how much!), but since he hadn't any earnings in 1961, while he was still in college, it would be advantageous from the tax standpoint to get a book contract and be paid the advance for it now, before the end of the year.

Well, I knew all about Nicklaus's brilliant record as an amateur, and I did have more than a casual hunch that he might well emerge as the next dominant figure in golf, when Arnold Palmer's era came to an end. As it turned out, that was the best bit of clairvoyance of my publishing life: I wish I had had the same sort of foresight when IBM stock was quoted at 51.

What did McCormack want as an advance for an unwritten book by a golfer who had yet to play in his first professional event? Mark said he realized he could only ask "modest money" for so speculative a venture, but anything was better than Jack's getting nothing in 1961, and he named a sum that was twice as much as the "modest" figure I had in mind. In view of what has happened since, both amounts seem ludicrously small now, but they didn't then. Still . . . the chance to sign up Nicklaus without having to compete with other publishers, and before the price escalated . . . pretty tempting if one believed in Nicklaus's future.

Suddenly I had an idea. While McCormack listened I picked up my telephone and had a call put through to the keenest golf enthusiast I knew among British book publishers, John Attenborough of Hodder & Stoughton, whose son, Michael, was not only a member of the firm but also a player on the British Walker Cup team. I explained the situation and told John that if he was inclined to take a flutter (as the British put it) on Nicklaus's potential, I was. Suppose I agreed to give McCormack the amount he was asking in exchange for our two firms' obtaining *world* English-language rights, instead of my simply getting the North American rights, which conventionally were the only ones granted to a U.S. publisher. Would Hodder & Stoughton be willing to take on the British Empire rights and pick up half of the risk?

I will always be impressed with the speed with which Attenborough said yes, and it bolstered my own resolve that much more. McCormack and I shook hands, and a contract was drawn and a check issued well before the December 31 deadline. Growing out of that small seed, Simon & Schuster has, over the past quarter of a century, published half a dozen Jack Nicklaus books, all very successful and several of them hugely so. It really is no wonder, since Jack became a superstar in 1962 in his very first year as a pro, winning the U.S. Open and the World Series of Golf, and has kept it up for more than two decades. No one has ever come even close to matching his record, and you can be pretty sure that no one ever will. Admittedly, there are so many wonderful young golfers now that even a standout can hardly dominate the present and future golf world the way Nicklaus did in the past; nevertheless, Jack's record is unbelievably spectacular. Apart from his 20 "major championship" titles, he has chalked up more than 70 tour victories plus 58 ties or second-place finishes, and he was clearly voted the Athlete of the Decade for the 1970's. His total book sales put to rout the sales of any other golf author, just as impressively as his playing record does the achievements of even the greatest other golfing immortals.

Naturally, having been lucky enough to hitch my wagon to such a star, I've been bonded to him as his intensely fanatical rooter, which is why I got so excited when he won the Masters that weekend to make his twentieth major. Also, we very old guys like to see old guys win in sports. What is more, my occasional contacts with him through the years have been very warm and pleasant, from editing his books to visiting him at his home in Palm Beach, where we played tennis together on his private grass court, to attending a Golden Bear annual business meeting, which Jack ran with a skill and flair that Lee Iacocca might envy. Golden Bear is the organization with which the many products that carry the Jack Nicklaus name are associated, including, of course, our books. Jack broke away from International Management Group, the Mark McCormack outfit, and formed his own corporation in 1970. He and his staff do a fine job administratively, and Jack himself is a figure of immense credibility when he endorses products on TV. He always insisted upon personal approval of all text and graphics in his books, and I understand that that's his policy in any advertising medium in which he's involved. Not only is he a giant of a sports hero, but also a very capable and honest and likable man.

Even though I'm now retired and won't be editing Jack's future books, I did touch base with him again on one occasion, just a couple of years ago. It had to do with the Skins Game, that made-for-television golf event that NBC devised and aired for the first time in 1983. In it four hand-picked stars play a round of 18 holes, the front nine being played on one weekend, and the back nine on the following one. There is a huge cash prize, and two factors bump up the stakes almost constantly. The first factor is simple. The cash prize per hole is augmented greatly after the first six holes, and then again after 12 holes, so that the final six holes are each being played for extremely large stakes, regardless of how well, or how badly, one has fared before then. The second factor, which is the real essence of the Skins Game, decrees that if instead of an outright win on a hole there is a tie for low, no money is won on that hole; rather, the money is added to the stakes on the next hole. The buildup is cumulative, should there be a tie for low ball on several holes in a row.

Clearly, with players of the calibre of Jack Nicklaus, Tom Watson, Gary Player, and Arnold Palmer, who were the contestants for the second Skins Game affair in 1984, this happens a lot. At least a couple of them were virtually sure to make par on any hole, which would make for a tie and a carryover, so scoring a birdie was practically a requirement in order to win a hole outright, and frequently even that wouldn't suffice because another player would score a birdie, too, and force a carryover. Although the event is a big-money TV production surrounded with hoopla that might perhaps offend a traditional sportsman, it is so fascinating to watch that it overcomes any such reluctance among golf purists. It combines the thrill of seeing enormous money hanging on a putt, time after time, with the unusual and highly pleasurable experience of seeing match play in championship golf for a change, involving man against man, as opposed to the more usual medal-play competition, where low total score wins.

Naturally I was rooting for my friend Nicklaus. But Jack hadn't been playing too well throughout 1984, and had also suffered a leg injury that hampered his swing to some extent. Right through the first nine holes he hardly figured at all in successful play, and whenever a Skins carryover took place, it invariably was because Player or Palmer or Watson had halved.

The first six holes carried a $10,000 prize each, the second six $20,000 each, and the final six $30,000 each, making a $360,000 pot for the 18 holes. At the end of the first nine holes, Tom Watson had swept all the money—$120,000 at that point—by virtue of winning a couple of holes early on and then winning a big carryover on the 9th hole. Player, Palmer, and Nicklaus had been shut out. It was simply Player and Palmer's bad luck that whenever either of them had seemed on the verge of winning a hole, somebody had halved him. They were playing just about as well as Watson, but the breaks were not going their way. Jack's situation was due more to the fact that he'd been playing miserable golf—for him.

The following weekend, play on the second nine holes began.

Starting with the 10th hole things went along much as they had on most of the front nine. Watson and Player were usually halving for low ball, with Palmer making a contribution to save a half now and then when one or the other of the two dominant figures faltered—but once again Jack Nicklaus wasn't figuring in things at all. He might as well not have been in the foursome. Still, no one had been able to win a hole outright over the first six holes of the back nine. By the 7th—the 16th hole on the course—three carry-overs of $20,000 each and three more of $30,000 each had accumulated, meaning that $150,000 in carryovers was riding on that hole, in addition to the $30,000 it was worth anyway. Just then, and really for the first time over the two weekends, Nicklaus sank a nasty, fairly long putt to halve the hole and save the carryover once more. He had to do it because two of the players had suffered reverses on that hole and were out of the running. So the carryover was now up to $180,000, with two holes to go, each worth $30,000.

Then, on the 17th, Nicklaus came through again, sinking a very tough putt after Player seemed sure to have low ball in hand and couldn't have been blamed for already counting his $210,000. Minutes later, on the 18th and last hole, after putting his drive into a difficult spot off the fairway, Jack pulled off a gorgeous long approach shot that left him only eight or 10 feet from the pin, and then, needing that putt for the birdie that would sweep the entire pot for the second nine—a little matter of $240,000—calmly stepped up and sank it! It was the biggest prize check of his entire career.

I was so thrilled about it—his gritty display on those last three holes after the gloomy first 15—that I telephoned him a couple of days later at home. After I congratulated him and marveled at the Garrison finish* he'd pulled off, Jack answered (and I could visual-

*For the benefit of readers who have never heard this expression, a Garrison finish is a horse race in which the winner comes from a long way behind to win by a nose in the last stride. Named for Snapper Garrison, a nineteenth-century U.S. jockey who is said to have done it all the time, the term can be found in your dictionary.

ize his grin as he said it), "Well, you know what Yogi Berra used to say, Peter. 'It isn't over until it's over!' "

That dictum was quoted so often in 1986, in connection with the Mets' miraculous late-innings heroics in the baseball playoffs and the World Series, that it almost seems trite today. But it didn't then, in 1984, and it never was more appropriate.

CHAPTER 8

The 1889 Super Bowl

A New York City holiday for
the Princeton-Yale game

My father, Frederick Schwed, Sr., was 12 years old in 1889. Born in Alabama but having spent his entire boyhood in New York City, he was, for reasons I have never completely fathomed, the most ardent of Princeton fans. A youngster who attended New York public schools and later City College, he had never even seen Princeton, let alone had any connection with the university, and I suspect his entire knowledge of it came from the sports pages. But somehow, by the time he was 12 he had adopted Princeton as *his* college, associating it with high romance, chivalry, and a kind of dashing spirit notably absent in his impression of the perhaps estimable enough Yale (stolid, dull, pipe-smoking chaps) or the perhaps not-to-be-despised Harvard (stony-faced, humorless book grinds). Clearly, there were no other colleges worth mentioning.

For in those early years of American football, college football was completely dominated by the Big Three, as Yale, Harvard, and Princeton were known. (There was no professional football—the first professional game between the two Pennsylvania towns of Latrobe and Jeanette wasn't until 1895, and the professional sport made no headway at all until well into the twentieth century.) In the year this story takes place, 1889, Caspar Whitney and Walter Camp picked the very first All-American team, consisting of 11 players; five from Princeton and three each from Harvard and Yale. It wasn't until more than 10 years later that players from such Midwestern universities as Michigan and Chicago gained grudging consideration, and in football terms the South and the West didn't exist at that time. Both Princeton and Yale were undefeated and had decisively beaten Harvard earlier that fall, so their game against each other was for the championship.

A large number of alumni of both colleges were living or working in the New York City area, and demand for tickets had far outstripped the modest seating accommodations that then existed on the two campuses. Further, the 250-mile round-trip journey between Princeton and New Haven made it virtually impossible for the students and fans from one college to attend a game at the other without making a full two-day affair out of it—and an uncomfortable one as well, since neither New Haven nor Princeton had proper lodgings for the thousands of visitors such games drew. Accordingly, the idea was born to situate the game in New York City, not only the approximate midpoint but a city that had a great many hotels and several large ballparks that could seat big crowds. It made good sense, and consequently from 1887 to 1896 the Princeton-Yale game became an annual November event—and what excitement it generated in the city! It truly was the Super Bowl of the latter part of the nineteenth century.

Each year the Yale contingent—players, coaches, managers, and just plain rooters—established its headquarters at the old Fifth Avenue Hotel at Madison Square at Twenty-third Street, and the Princeton partisans took over the Murray Hill Hotel, a little farther uptown. Starting at ten o'clock on the morning of the game, a staggeringly long procession of carriages festooned with blue or orange-and-black bunting started up Fifth Avenue to the strains of "Bulldog! Bulldog!" or "Old Nassau." The men in the carriages flaunted their respective college colors, wearing ties and scarves of the appropriate hue; the women wore dresses and coats whose color didn't clash with violets, in the one case, or in the other, chrysanthemums. Along the entire length of Fifth Avenue the fashionable department stores, hotels, and restaurants celebrated the occasion and showed their impartiality by flying large banners for both universities (unless the owner was an alumnus of Princeton or Yale). Finally the parade would reach the uptown destination where the game would take place; in 1889 it was the Berkeley Oval, situated on Fifth Avenue just north of Central Park. In other years games were played at the old Polo Grounds, or Manhattan Field, or Eastern Park, in Brooklyn. In the last case the carriage procession must have wended its way across the Brooklyn Bridge.

At the ballpark large wicker hampers filled with sumptuous luncheon delicacies provided by the hotels and gourmet provisioners—and accompanied by lots of liquid refreshment—were unloaded from each carriage. A great communal picnic took place on the grass and under the trees surrounding the grandstand. This day was a party day, no matter who finally won the game, and everyone would later return downtown for an all-night celebration.

Still, for most people, including my 12-year-old father, the important thing was the game itself. That year, as in years past, reserved seats had been completely commandeered by the Yale and Princeton student body and alumni, who were entitled to apply early for them and would no more have thought of scalping their precious tickets than they would have considered scalping their nearest and dearest. But as is still the case today with certain enormously popular sporting events, such as the World Series, a modest block of unreserved seats was always put aside to be sold to the general public on a first-come-first-served basis on the morning of the game, and this is where my father's story starts.

Pop received a weekly allowance from his own pop, and he also earned a small amount on summer jobs. Throughout 1889 he regularly, if painfully, saved a little each week in order to build up the vast sum that would be needed to buy a general-admission ticket to the Princeton-Yale game, once the great day actually rolled around. I don't know how much money he needed—probably a couple of dollars—but in those days that was a lot of money for a young boy, and not inconsiderable for an adult. It would buy you a full meal in an excellent restaurant.

Pop had the required sum, and he knew he had to be in line early in the morning to be sure that the limited stock of such tickets wasn't exhausted before he got to the window. Kickoff wasn't scheduled until early afternoon, but the box-office window would open at nine o'clock in the morning. Some particularly fanatical cohorts would bring blankets and pillows and actually sleep on the ground in front of the window in order to be among the first to get into the stands, but that wasn't really necessary, and, more to the point, Pop's mother wouldn't let him do that. But she did make some sandwiches and cocoa and set the alarm for five A.M. so that, with a little hustle, Pop would be able to join the line before six o'clock, more than an hour before sunrise.

Armed with a long, noisy horn carefully painted in tiger style with orange-and-black stripes, and bundled up in a wild orange-and-black scarf with knitted cap to match, Pop made his way uptown on the trolley hours before the big, fashionable carriage parade was scheduled even to start its long path up Fifth Avenue. Well before six he had a firmly established place in line, no more than about thirtieth from the window, so he knew he was in no danger of having the supply of tickets run out on him. He now had a three-hour wait until the window opened, however, so he started to look around for a diversion. He did not have far to look.

Directly behind him in the line were a man and a woman, both in their middle twenties. On any other occasion Pop would have thought them a nice-looking couple, but the man wore a jaunty blue feather with a white Y impressed upon it in the band of his hat, along with a blue-and-white striped tie, and she had a bouquet of blue violets pinned to her coat lapel. The enemy!

Nobody can be more noisy, more raucous, and generally more objectionable in a decorous society than a 12-year-old boy who has decided that the occasion justifies his making a career out of being noisy, raucous, and generally objectionable. In between bites of his sandwiches and sips of his cocoa, Pop favored the couple with his unalterable views on the glories and splendor of the Princeton football team and the inadequacies and hopelessness of the Yale eleven. Fortunately, he shrilled at the top of his voice in between intermittent blasts on his horn, these truths would be revealed to the entire world when those titans of nobility, Princeton's redoubtable Hector Cowan, Edgar Allen Poe, and Snake Ames, made mincemeat of the highly overrated Yale stars, Pudge Heffelfinger, Charley Gill, and Amos Alonzo Stagg. Derision combined with bravado was Pop's oratorical style, and it didn't slow him down one whit when the Yale couple quietly confined their rebuttals to pointing out that the Yale team also was undefeated, and that comparative scores of earlier games against other joint rivals indicated that this game would be a toss-up. Pop took little notice of their friendly good manners and continued with his show of rampant defiance.

Finally the box office window opened and the line moved forward. As Pop neared the window he dug down in his pocket for his precious money, and it wasn't where he had so carefully tucked it just before leaving the house! Frantic, he searched all his other pockets, but it was hopeless: he knew which one it should be in. Somehow, somewhere, he had lost the money or it had been stolen. The line had come to a complete standstill as Pop continued his desperate, futile search, and many angry cries of "Move on! Let's go!" came from behind. The tears had long since passed the point of welling up in Pop's eyes. Now they were flowing down both cheeks in a torrent.

At this point the young man with the Y feather in his hat gently pushed my father slightly aside, stepped up to the window, and said, "Three, please." He turned to Pop, thrust one of the tickets into his hand, and said, "Princeton shouldn't lose as loyal a rooter as you are." Without waiting for the thanks of the emotion-shattered and for once mute boy, the young man tucked the young woman's hand under his arm and moved off hurriedly. I imagine that, sympathetic as he was to Pop's distress, he could not bear the distinct possibility that Pop might tag along and sit next to him throughout the game.

When my father told me this story, he finished it this way.

"As you know, I was fortunate enough to be able to send my sons to Princeton, and right through my life, whenever Yale and Princeton meet each other, I have continued to root for Princeton. But any time Yale is playing some *other* college, I'm a one hundred percent Yale man!"

CHAPTER 9

The World Series Without Television

*Giants vs. Yankees: a tale
of two schoolboys in 1921*

It was a natural outgrowth for my grandchildren, Alex and Emily, having been fanatical television viewers from their earliest *Sesame Street* days, to become almost equally fanatical baseball television viewers. In 1986, whenever an adult usurped the television set to watch the Mets coast to the National League East title and then battle for their lives in the playoffs, they watched as much as they could until it was time to go to bed. They didn't see much of the World Series because all of the Series games, including the weekend ones, were held at night, more is the shame. Still, they were able to follow the heroic exploits of their team, the Mets, in the following day's newspapers and revel in their favorites' eventual triumph.

I liked to talk baseball with them because it gave me a special opportunity to flaunt my knowledge—a grandfather's prerogative. One day, for instance, in a game on the tube, a runner was trapped between bases, and the basemen had to exchange four or five throws before they were able to run him down.

I said, "Well, that worked out all right, but they did it all wrong. They might have missed the runner, having had so many chances to make a bad throw or bad catch, and if there had been another runner on base at the time, he probably could have advanced to the next base while all that was going on."

I explained that I knew this because a man named Branch Rickey, who probably knew more about baseball than anyone who ever lived, told me the right way. Mr. Rickey was a wonderful man who could have had any career but chose to make baseball his life. First he was a player, then he became a coach, a manager, a general manager, and finally an owner, and he was immensely successful at everything. It was Mr. Rickey who broke the prejudice against black baseball players in the big leagues by signing Jackie Robinson to play with the Brooklyn Dodgers. Rickey's choice of Robinson was brilliant: Robinson never truckled to anyone, and his essential dignity and style had almost as much to do with paving the way for the complete acceptance of black players as did his wonderful performances on the field. Branch Rickey also invented the now compulsory batting helmet that has done so much to protect players from serious injury and even death.

I knew Mr. Rickey well because I published a book that he wrote with a fine photographer and artist, Robert Riger, called *The American Diamond*; as Mr. Rickey's editor I saw him quite frequently. One day while the book was still being written he took me out to Shea Stadium to see a game between his team at that time, the St. Louis Cardinals, and the Mets. Throughout the game he kept up a running stream of observations that were eye-openers even to an old-time fan like me who thought he knew his baseball pretty well. I was particularly impressed by what he had to say at one point when a runner got trapped between bases, and I made sure he put it into the book he was writing.

"The rundown is possibly the most neglected defensive play in the game. Let us say that the catcher has the ball with the runner trapped between third and home. The first thing the catches does is to start toward the runner with all the speed he has, and instead of making the fake motion up high and above

the waistline, goes completely through with his arm swing. Basemen generally do not know the effect on the base runner of completely carrying through the fake throw. It brings the runner to a dead stop. The catcher's running speed increases instantly and frequently results in the catcher making the tag and never throwing the ball at all. When, in a major league game, you see the ball thrown back and forth three or four times, you can very well know that the basemen don't know anything about how to catch the runner on a rundown. The full sweep of the arm on the part of a baseman is the key to the quick rundown and saves the play because the succeeding runner cannot advance as he might on a long rundown."

"That's interesting, Grandpa," Emily said, "and I can see how it would work even in softball games on the beach. You were actually at the game when Mr. Rickey told you that? You weren't watching television? I didn't know you ever went to games. Everybody I know, like you and Daddy and Alex and the other kids, watches on television."

"Baseball is a lot older than television, dear, and so am I," I said. "Certainly, I went to lots and lots of games years ago, and I'm darned if I quite know why I don't stir myself and go sometimes now. Actually being there is the right way to see baseball, and although watching on television can be fun, it isn't the same thing. As a matter of fact, do you know what else isn't as old as baseball either, but is a lot older than television? And was lots of fun before television came along? Radio—that's what, and now I'm remembering a thing that happened to me and a friend of mine when we were just about your age. It was at the time of the 1921 World Series between the old New York Giants and the New York Yankees. My friend Bobby and I were just grade-school kids then, like you and Alex now, and it was the most exciting thing we ever did together." And I told her the following story.

Baseball fever was at its height that year, particularly in New York, which had not only the championship teams of both leagues but also individual heroes who were well on their way to becoming legends. In particular there was Babe Ruth, who had been a brilliant pitcher for the Boston Red Sox but who now played right field for the Yankees so that he could play—and bat—every day. The Babe was hitting home runs at a pace that had never been seen before. Both teams had wonderful pitchers: the Giants boasted Art Nehf, Phil Douglas, and Virgil Barnes; the Yankees had Waite Hoyt, Carl Mays, and Bob Shawkey. The prospect was for a great Series, but unless you were one of the lucky 35,000 or so people who could be squeezed into the Polo Grounds, where all the games took place—Yankee Stadium wasn't built until 1923—you had to be satisfied to read about the games later in the newspapers.

You could stand in front of certain shop windows for a few hours each afternoon (no night games back then) and see the half-inning scores posted as a game progressed. Those stores received the information by telephone or from a ticker tape. That way, every 10 minutes or so you at least learned how things were going generally for your team, but there was no way for those not actually at the ballpark to keep abreast of the game via live, play-by-play reporting.

Well, that year, for the first time, there was a new possibility, but only after a fashion. Radio was being tested, and station WJZ in New York had decided to broadcast the Series in a three-way hook-up with station KDKA in Pittsburgh and WBZ in East Springfield, Massachusetts. It's hard to think for whose benefit they were doing this, since virtually no one had ever seen, let alone owned a radio receiving set, but if they were going to run experimental tests, you can see that this promised to be an interesting one.

My friend Bobby, a sixth-grader like me, was a wizard at scientific and mechanical things and an insatiable reader of publications like *Popular Mechanics.* This was not a passion we shared, but there was another passion we did share—big-league baseball—and when Bobby heard that a New York station was going to broadcast the Series by radio, he told me he thought he could build a receiver that could pick it up from our homes on Long

Island. I watched, fascinated, as he constructed the first crystal galena radio receiving set that I or anyone else I knew had ever seen. I remember that the condenser was made by wrapping a long length of copper wire in a coil around a cardboard tube we took out of a roll of toilet paper. I don't recall much else except that Bobby had to probe the lump of galena constantly with a wire feeler; this enabled him to pick up the broadcast being carried to his headphones. There were a number of lapses, but Bobby eventually got the hang of the thing in test airings the station sent out in the days before the Series. Soon he wasn't losing contact at all, but it kept him pretty busy. That opened the door for me: I had a louder voice than Bobby and was less shy, and we each had a role in the plan we were hatching.

We got some large pieces of cardboard and made up a dozen signs in glowing colors, which the friendly village shopkeepers in our small town allowed us to display prominently in their windows the week before the great event we had in mind. Each sign read: WORLD SERIES, GAME 3, GIANTS VS. YANKEES, SATURDAY, OCTOBER 7TH AT 2:30 P.M. PLAY-BY-PLAY ACCOUNT WHILE THE GAME IS ACTUALLY IN PROGRESS, AS RECEIVED BY RADIO. EVERYBODY WELCOME, NO CHARGE. BRING YOUR CAMP CHAIRS, BLANKETS, OR WHATEVER TO THE GROUNDS ON THE SOUTH SIDE OF THE SCHWED HOUSE ON GREENWOOD AVENUE.

Why had we chosen the third game? Because it was the only game for which we could pull our stunt legitimately. It was a nine-game series then, unless one team won five games before the Series went the limit, and the first two games were scheduled for the preceding Thursday and Friday. That Saturday was the only day we'd not be in school during the game (baseball wasn't played on Sundays back then). By the following Saturday, unless the teams went the full nine games (they didn't), the Series would be over, so this third game had to be it. You may ask if it didn't occur to us to play hooky for at least one other game? Certainly it did, but we could hardly play hooky before a crowd of more than 200 people—probably including some school teachers—which was the size of the crowd we drew that Saturday. Probably we did play hooky for another game, but if we did, we didn't advertise it. I suspect we did because doing so at World Series time started then to become an American institution. As Tom Weir of *USA Today* recently put it, the fact that most games are played at night these days—to baseball's shame, *all* of the 1986 Series games were at night—is cheating today's kids of one of the joys of childhood: "They'll never get to play the best fall sport ever invented—World Series hooky."

Be that as it may, that Saturday turned out to be a beautiful day, and the crowd, half adults and half youngsters, was just about equally divided in their affections for the two New York teams. The Yankees had already won the first two games when first Waite Hoyt and then Carl Mays shut out the Giants without a run, so by the third game Giant fans were desperately waiting for their team to burst loose. In the seventh inning, with the score tied 4-4, they did just that, scoring eight runs in that inning to win the game 13-5. They eventually took the Series as well, five games to three, as their star pitchers, Phil Douglas and Art Nehf, turned the tables on Mays and Hoyt in the final two games, both brilliant pitching duals. It is to be regretted—or it was then—that the Yankees didn't win one of them so that there would have been a final, deciding ninth game on the following Saturday, but it was not to be.

But that third game, the one we did broadcast, was a slugfest, and Bobby, perched at a table on our porch, probed the galena frantically while trying to make out the quite factual description coming over the air waves. Bobby would give me the tense report that "Ruth flied out to Irish Meusel," and I would jazz it up in translation to the crowd by bellowing through my microphone something like: "The Babe's up! Oh, oh—he's really got hold of one! This may be it! No, Irish is fading back right up against the fence. He's under it! He's got it!"

You may wonder how I, who of course had never been exposed to the colorful play-by-play depictions that came along in later years on radio, could have managed this sort of thing. Well, I was an omnivorous reader of every word in the newspaper sports sections, and in those days the great sports writers like Grantland Rice and George Trevor were given columns daily in which to wax lyrical, and wax lyrical they did. I not only picked up intensified sports enthusiasm from them, but also sports vernacular.

After the game was over, a lot of people hung around to congratulate us both on what we had pulled off, but there was a lot more interest in Bobby's radio receiver, and how he made it, than there was in my oratory. The fact is that Bobby was asked to take over a science section one day the following week, and explain the construction and operation of it all. But no talent scout radio station ever got in touch with me about stepping into the shoes that might have been mine, but which turned out in subsequent years to be filled by my admittedly pretty good successors, such as Bill Stern and Mel Allen and Red Barber. Ah well, it's an unfair world.

CHAPTER 10

My Old Man

Winner take all

Living on the south shore of Long Island when I was a boy was heaven for our essentially masculine, sports-minded family. My two brothers and I were not interested in horses and the racetrack, but my father made up for us. We weren't more than a few miles from all of the three Long Island tracks, Belmont, Aqueduct, and Jamaica, and they all held a racing season, so for a good portion of the year my dad could be found at the betting windows of one or the other of them. But they were by no means the only sporting attractions our part of the world offered, and there was hardly a weekend in summer when the siren call of an event wouldn't lure at least one or more of us.

For me, the equivalent of my father's making a second home at the track was my constant attendance at whatever was going on at the West Side Tennis Club in Forest Hills, and plenty was going on in those years. I started going to the National singles championships in 1920, which was the year when Big Bill Tilden won for the first time, and I saw him win the first title and those for the next five years as well. No one really threatened Tilden's reign during that period to the point where anyone thought he would lose, although Little Bill Johnston did make it close a couple of times on pure spunk. Lots of us found ourselves rooting for Johnston in certain years because he was so small compared to Tilden, and because he was the underdog.

Then, in the middle of Tilden's winning streak, along came Helen Wills in 1923 to become equally dominant in the women's part of the tournaments. Miss Wills won the U.S. women's title every year from 1923 through 1931 except for 1926 and 1930, when she did not compete in the tournament. So as a boy I regularly saw the two players whom, until very recent years, most people would have rated as the greatest of their respective sexes— and many still would.

As if the singles championships were not enough, the Davis Cup matches were also staged at the West Side Tennis Club, against Japan in 1921 and against Australasia in 1922 and 1923. With Tilden and Johnston playing for the United States, the results were a foregone conclusion, but the contests were fun. It was only a twenty-minute ride from our town to Forest Hills on the Long Island Railroad, so I saw every match.

It was even easier to get to the Inwood Country Club, to which my parents belonged, and in 1923 the U.S. Open golf championships were held there. I could ride my bicycle to Inwood, which enabled me to see Bobby Jones win his very first major championship and get his autograph on a program. I already had Tilden's autograph and a baseball signed by Babe Ruth, and they were my most prized possessions for years. One summer vacation a few years later when I came home from prep school, however, none of them could be found. I always suspected it must have been the work of a Black Hand Gang or something equally sinister: my mother denied that spring housecleaning could have had anything to do with the disappearance.

Only once did I get to see another of the marvelous sport spectacles that took place comparatively nearby: the international Westchester Cup polo match between the United States and Great Britain of 1924. The Meadow Brook Club wasn't as close or easily reached as the Inwood Country Club, but the family had a car, which was unusual then, and a combination man-about-the-house, gardener, and chauffeur who could drive us on those quite rare occasions when using the car made sense. This was one such occasion, and the whole family went off to see another immortal from that Golden Age of Sport, Thomas Hitchcock, Jr., lead the United States polo team to a solid victory.

The fact is that there rarely was any real need to use an automobile back then. If we wanted to go to a baseball game in New York, the train and the subway would get us from door to grandstand seat in an hour and a half. Or you could leave home in midmorning, make your way to the Polo Grounds, see a game, which usually lasted only an hour and a half to two hours (today, for a variety of reasons, they invariably last three hours or more), and easily be back home in time for dinner. Who needed a car?

One event for which we did need the car was the Princeton-Yale football game each fall. The Big Three games—Princeton vs. Harvard, Yale vs. Princeton, and Harvard vs. Yale—continued to be the biggest thing in football right into the 1920's, which is the era we're remembering, and for Princeton rooters like ourselves the Yale game was more important than the Harvard one. Also, the trip to and from Cambridge in alternate years for the Harvard game was an absurdly long one to think of undertaking. The round trip to Princeton or to New Haven for the Yale game was quite strenuous enough. Let's suppose the game took place at Princeton.

The first leg would be to drive in the car along the only road leading from Long Island to Manhattan, Queens Boulevard. Although that portion of the trip was only about twenty miles, it took roughly an hour, for nobody drove very fast then. After crossing the Queensboro Bridge, we would have to wend our way south and west across Manhattan to reach the ferry, way downtown, somewhere around Liberty Street, and that took the better part of another hour. Then you waited for the ferry that would transport you and your car across the Hudson River. There were no bridges or tunnels for automobile traffic between New York and New Jersey in those days—only the tunnel carrying Pennsylvania

Railroad trains. Why didn't we take the train? I'm not sure, for it certainly would have been simpler and faster. I was a young boy then and wasn't making decisions for the family, but I think that the annual trip, the way my parents planned it, was a sort of wonderful weekend vacation for us all. It was no pressurized one-day expedition.

It hardly could have been, for what with waiting for a ferry and the cross-Hudson passage, it now became a matter of almost three hours since leaving home before we were finally in New Jersey. Eureka! But where were we in New Jersey? In Jersey City, that's where, and still about forty miles from Princeton. The only route there was the old Lincoln Highway, which passed through every town on the map, with stoplights all the way. The forty-mile trip added something like another couple of hours, which would make it five hours from beginning to end, not counting time needed to park the car, eat the basket lunch we brought along—we were almost the first of the "tailgate set," long before there were any tailgates, and ate, picnic style, on the grass—and get to our seats. If you work backward in time you will see that in order to be there for a one o'clock kickoff we had to leave home no later than seven in the morning. The game took the better part of three hours, so we wouldn't have gotten back home before ten o'clock at night, not having had any dinner, if we had tried to do it in one day. It certainly wouldn't have been much fun, no matter how good the game turned out to be.

Pop solved this problem by always making it a two-day affair. What would be absurd today made very good sense then and turned a potential horror into such an enjoyable experience that my mother, no ardent football fan, always got great pleasure out of coming along. We would leave Long Island at about noon on Friday, the day before the game, and drive the extra nine miles past Princeton on to Trenton, a surprisingly pleasant city back then and one that boasted a splendid hotel, the Stacy-Trent. There we had dinner, perhaps saw a show, and spent the night, making our leisurely way back to Princeton the following morning a couple of hours before the game so that we'd have time for our picnic lunch. After the game we would start back for home and would pass through New York City at about nine o'clock—too late for dinner but not too late to stop at a new restaurant-delicatessen that was just then becoming famous, Reuben's, where a most marvelous hamper of sandwiches, cheesecake, and hot drinks that my father had previously ordered would be waiting for us. That was eaten on the final leg of the trip home, and I, the baby of the group, fell happily asleep before the cheesecake was served—happily, that is, if Princeton had won the football game.

In alternate years, when the game was played at New Haven, we did more or less the same thing. No ferry ride was involved then, but the trip was some 30 miles longer, so the time span was pretty much the same, and New Haven's Taft Hotel was just about as good as the Stacy-Trent.

Ensconced cosily in an easy chair in front of a television set where, what with college football on Saturdays and professional football on Sundays and Monday nights, you can see something like 10 games in any week in the fall if you're so inclined, you may indeed have cause to wonder. Why would anybody look back with such obvious relish on going to all that trouble, and spending all that time and money, to see one game?

Football today, dominated like so many sports by television, offers such a supersaturation of goodies that one is likely not to care very much about any individual contest. You just let the whole thing wash over you. While you may maintain a special interest in a particular team and follow its progress with some excitement, there's so much competition for your attention that the old focus on major rivalries once a year is nothing like what it was. You're hardly aware of what happened two weeks ago, let alone what happened a year or two ago. Quick, now! Who played in the Super Bowl last year? The year before last?

Back in the time I'm writing about, when there was no television and no professional football to speak of, when few college teams could challenge the Big Three, real fans were very aware of the three games that took place each year in the round-robin rivalry of Yale, Harvard, and Princeton. They could tell you who won not only the previous year but also the half-dozen years before that, and the real zealots could rattle off the scores! Those games were once-a-year festivities worth going to considerable trouble about, not that different in magnitude from Christmas and New Year's. My father claimed (half seriously) that he sent his sons to Princeton primarily to secure good tickets to the Yale game, and he made the hotel reservations in Trenton or New Haven months before the game each year.

Those football games were innocent sporting affairs that Pop converted into attractive family outings we all shared. But my dad was also often a free-swinging individualist who extended his passion for sports and gambling into any area where he felt he could get a good bet down. There was that time in 1919 when he left us all to go off to Toledo, Ohio, to see a young slugger named Jack Dempsey fight Jess Willard for the heavyweight boxing championship of the world.

Pop simply had to see that fight, and that year he was really in the chips, as he often was. People with major gambling skills and temperaments have their ups and downs. The year 1919 was an up year for my father, so together with a number of other rich men he hired a private railroad car that would carry them all to Toledo in real style. A major attraction for my father was that there would be a good, high-stakes bridge game in the car, because George S. Kaufman, Herbert Bayard Swope, and Chico Marx had signed up. My father was one of the best auction bridge players in the country, and of course played for very high stakes. He did a lot better at the bridge table than he did at the racetrack. Pop knew all three other men not only as the important figures they were in the theater, the press, and the movies, but even better as excellent bridge players who, like him, didn't play for pennies. It promised to be a swell train trip to Ohio and back, and, incidentally, there was the Willard-Dempsey fight to look forward to.

But when the train pulled out of the station it turned out that something had prevented Chico Marx from making it, and there was no one else in the car with the requisite combined ability and bankroll to make a suitable fourth. A number of people had started up a crap game at one end of the car, and although my old man really didn't enjoy dice at all, it was, as they say, the only game in town. So he joined in.

At about two-thirty in the morning, speeding through the fields of western Pennsylvania, he found himself in an embarrassing position. He was $300,000 ahead. Such a winner can hardly stand up and yawn and say, "Well, time to go—the little woman is staying up for me." It's extremely hard to quit a game under such circumstances unless you're playing in a gambling casino with strangers, which was not the case. Pop finally solved the problem this way.

When it became his turn to roll the dice next he paused and instead offered a proposition. "Look," he said, "this game can go on all night and you may win your money back. On the other hand I may win twice as much. There's no way of knowing, and I'll offer you a much better chance to get even. Two flips of a coin, heads or tails each time for the whole pot. If I win the first flip the stake is six hundred thousand for the second flip. If you win *either* flip I lose it all, but if I win *both* flips you'll have to get up a syndicate because I'll be owed one million two hundred thousand dollars. I know you're all aware of what the odds are with respect to winning two flips of a coin in a row—they're three to one against it happening. I'm offering you the best gamble you're likely to encounter in a long time—maybe forever. So what about it? At least no matter how it comes out we can all go to bed and get some sleep and be able to enjoy the fight."

After some discussion the players agreed to Pop's proposal and the train conductor flipped a coin and let it land on the floor of the car. It would be nice to draw out this story to make it even more dramatic, and write that he won that first flip and that $600,000 was riding on the second, but he didn't. He lost the first flip and went off to bed.

This was such an extraordinary story, even for my flamboyant dad, that for some time I wondered if it really happened just the way he described it, or was it at least exaggerated to some extent. But years later I met Herbert Bayard Swope, then the publisher of the old *World*, and he confirmed it.

My father wasn't really a dyed-in-the-wool fight fan, but he did attend a big fight now and then. He went alone—for some reason he never took any of us. Maybe Mother disapproved, and possibly he himself thought the sport a seedy one and not the type of romantic sport that he liked to share with his kids. I do, however, remember one other boxing tale he told me, and while this one has nobody to vouch for its veracity—and it seems pretty wild—I never caught my father out in telling us something about himself that didn't actually happen.

He knew a lot of sporting characters, and one with whom he had a superficial acquaintanceship was a fairly highly ranked welterweight fighter named Paddy. Paddy was never going to be a champion, but he was a decent, workmanlike performer with an enthusiastic local following.

One night Paddy attended a fight that was being held between the two chief contenders for the light-heavyweight title. The winner was to get a shot at the title. That made it a big fight, and the arena was packed: an added inducement was that a substantial part of the proceeds were slated to be given to a local charity. But half an hour before the fight was to begin, one of the fighters slipped on something while taking warm-up exercises in his dressing room and sprained his ankle so badly that it was obvious he wouldn't be able to go on.

The promoter of the fight was desperate, and he spotted Paddy sitting in a front row near the ring. He beckoned to Paddy to join him and then led him to the back of the arena.

"Paddy," he said, "we can't put the fight on as scheduled, and apart from returning all the money including the take for the hospital, this crowd is going to go crazy if we just call off every thing. I know it's short notice and I don't know if you're in peak condition and I realize you'll be giving away something like a twenty-five- or thirty-pound weight advantage, but could you do it? There's five thousand dollars for you if you can last three rounds and fifteen hundred no matter what." This took place around 1910, and both sums were considerable for Paddy, who was not much more than a good club fighter. He considered the matter for a moment or two and then went off to a dressing room to don trunks and put on the gloves.

The crowd was disappointed, but Paddy was popular and there were no screams of "Money back!" But from the sound of the bell for the first round it was obvious that Paddy was not only badly outweighed but also badly overmatched. His opponent punched him mercilessly and at will: Paddy was floored three times in the first round but always made it back to his feet and tried to keep fighting. And so it went through two more rounds with Paddy taking more and more of a beating and hitting the canvas another three times.

Because the promoter had promised Paddy more money if he lasted three rounds, and he wanted that outcome not only to give the crowd its money's worth but also because he was sincerely obligated to Paddy, the promotor had told the referee not to stop the fight short of three rounds if he could possibly justify keeping it going. Paddy was taking a frightful beating that would normally have impelled a referee to step in, but he kept getting up and trying to do his best. Finally, just barely surviving the third round, he staggered out for the fourth, made no attempt to protect his chin, and was knocked out cold by an uppercut. In falling he broke his collarbone and sustained a leg fracture.

Some time later my father ran into Paddy on the street. He was no longer having to use crutches but he still used a cane and the marks from the fight were clearly evident on his face.

"Paddy," said my father, "I was so sorry to hear about what happened to you during the fight, and I understand that your hospital expenses used up all of the five thousand you were paid for lasting three rounds. Is that true?"

Paddy looked at my old man through eyes that were still somewhat puffed up, and spoke through lips that were equally so.

"That's right, Fred," he said, "but you know the old saying: Easy come, easy go."

CHAPTER 11

The Sport of Kings

Horse players die broke

It has been said that all horse players die broke, and my father was no exception, although, to be fair, it was more the stock market and the Great Depression that finally did him in. Still, Fred Sr. had a lot of fun while the going was good, and a healthy chunk of it came from his love affair with the racetrack. It was intense enough that he actually owned a small racing stable for a few of his palmier years.

Pop never owned more than three or four horses at a time, and none of them made much of a mark in racing annals, but he did come close on one occasion. Both in making his bets and in purchasing a race horse, his prime consideration was the horse's breeding. He would never bid for an established horse on the basis of his record or promise. That was for the real owners whose lives were devoted to building and maintaining racing stables. Buying a horse already known as a likely winner was expensive. My father, for whom owning a horse or two was no more than a hobby, preferred to attend the yearling auction sales of untested colts that were held each year at the Saratoga meeting. These very young horses, unraced to date, on the whole didn't fetch more at auction than Pop was willing to spend, and he figured his knowledge of the stud book gave him as good a chance to pick a winner as the next bidder.

Each August my father took the entire family to Saratoga, where we all stayed in one of those two glorious, huge old hotels that dominated the main street of the town in those years, the Grand National and the United States. Saratoga was a lovely place to spend a summer month in the most elegant of surroundings, and each year my mother and we boys found plenty of diverting things to do while Pop more or less lived at the track.

One year—if must have been either 1917 or 1918—my eldest brother, Fred Jr., accompanied him to the yearling auction sale: both John and I were too young, and it wasn't my mother's idea of the way to pass a beautiful day in a delightful town. But Fred was about 15 years old and the idea interested him; he was old enough to be allowed into the sale, so Pop took him along. My father gave him a small orientation course in the genealogy of the young horses that were slated to be auctioned off and explained that they usually could be bought for sums ranging from $1,000 to $2,000. He did, however, confide to Freddy that he was determined to buy a particular colt that had caught his eye. The colt's sire had been Fair Play, a pet favorite of my father's and a horse on which he had cashed in a lot of winning tickets in the past. Added to that, the yearling's dam was Mahubar, whose own sire, Rock Sand, had won the British Triple Crown back in 1903. For a man who placed his reliance on breeding, the auspices were irresistible, and Pop told Fred he was prepared to plunge if necessary. Very rarely did the bidding in the auction reach $2,500, but Pop said he was prepared to go that high and might even stretch and bid higher, possibly to $3,000. He was going to buy this horse and that was the end of it. Freddy listened, and having for once no comment to make, made none.

When the horse was finally put up for auction, the bidding was brisk, as was expected, and quickly ran up to a couple of thousand dollars, but at $2,500 all the bidders dropped away except only two, my father and a quiet, inconspicuous fellow whom Pop had never seen before. Bit by bit they bid against each other. My father was thinking that if they had not already gone crazy they were getting there. For bidding in increments of $100, they were already close to $4,000—an unheard-of figure. (Remember, these were pre-1920 dollars.) The quiet man bid $4,000, and my father, ever one inclined to take Fate by the throat and chance winning or losing it all, frowned, shot Freddy a quick side-glance, and called, "Five thousand!" There was a lengthy pause while the quiet man seemed frozen—Freddy certainly was—and then he raised his program to signal another $100 and bring the price to $5,100. Pop decided that there had to be a limit to lunacy and dropped out, much to Fred's relief, as he later told me.

Afterward my father learned that the quiet man was a representative of Samuel Riddle, owner of one of the most prestigious and richest racing stables in the United States. Mr. Riddle obviously had fallen in love with this particular colt too; feeling that the competition might be unusually keen and not wanting to be seen bidding himself, he had sent a delegate with instructions to go to $5,000, a sum that would surely top any bidding. The quiet man had taken it upon himself to exceed Mr. Riddle's instructions by that last $100, and one can only wonder what would have happened had Pop tried one more gasp at lunacy and bid $5,200. By this time you may have guessed the punch line to this tale. My father would have owned Man O'War!

Well, Pop may have been right about genealogy being all-important in buying yearlings, but his own genes didn't have any effect upon his children as far as their interest in horse racing is concerned. Fred probably was cured of any tendency that day at Saratoga when he saw $5,000 almost go down the drain, and my other brother, John, and I never were bitten by the bug. I've taken my wife, Toni, to a track once or twice when we've been on vacation in a location where racing was one of the major attractions, but that's about it. There is, however, one family occasion that takes place once a year: on the day of the Kentucky Derby, Toni and I are likely to turn on the television set in the late afternoon and watch it. A funny thing happened in 1980.

It adds an extra fillip of interest when watching a race to have a small bet down and be able to root for a horse. So it's my practice to make my one annual visit to an offtrack betting office in New York a day or two before the Derby and put down a bet. It's understood that I will share the winnings, if any, with any members of my family who happen to be watching that day. Prior to 1980 there never had been any winnings, although we'd come close a couple of times. But I always bet to win, not place or show, and I never select favorites, wanting to get a price if I ever do win. That combination of betting principles means that if you do win you win substantially, but you don't win too often.

In 1980 I placed my bet the Friday afternoon before the race at an OTB office. Suddenly, somebody thrust a microphone in front of my mouth and inquired, "What horse did you bet on, sir, and why?" I didn't know who my interrogator was, but I'm a cooperative fellow, so I replied to the effect that I was a staunch feminist and so I had bet on the only filly in the race.

That night, on a major television network's six o'clock news, there I was in a pre-Kentucky Derby segment telling the world my choice.

This story has two endings, one good and one bad. First the good one: the filly, Genuine Risk, did indeed win! The odds shown on the tote board at Louisville showed that she paid off at about 13 to 1, which meant that I would collect $260 for my $20 bet! Toni and I were the only ones around watching that day, so we should each pick up $130 of found money!

Now for the bad news. When I went to the offtrack betting office to collect, I received only about half of what we expected. The odds at an OTB office have nothing to do with those shown on the tote board at the track; they merely reflect the odds established by the money bet on each horse at the OTB windows. A lot of people had played Genuine Risk at the OTB in New York—many more than at Louisville. Could it be that in New York City horse-playing women heard my pronouncement on the news the evening before the race, rushed out the following morning and jumped on my bandwagon, thus driving the OTB odds way down? If there's a better explanation, I've not yet learned what it is.

CHAPTER 12

The Awful Truth

The big leagues never wanted me

Seeing how interested I've always seemed to be in the world of sport, it's not illogical that my children sometimes asked me if I played the games they were playing when I myself was their age, and whether I was any good at them. The awful truth is that I did play them, but until I was well into my teens I was more of a loser than anything else. You see, I was such a fat little boy when I went away to boarding school at the age of 12 that I was almost a circus freak, being just five feet tall and weighing almost 190 pounds! You can imagine what kind of athlete a boy who could hardly waddle must have been. Having lost that surplus tonnage one summer through a simple diet called starvation, by my final school years and throughout my college career I became a fair enough athlete at dormitory and intramural levels, and even played varsity-calibre tennis. Later, in my twenties, I actually achieved national ranking in badminton, a sport you will read about in the next chapter. But when I was a young underformer at my school, Lawrenceville, I can only recall two experiences that, even if they didn't quite qualify me for the school Hall of Shame, didn't make a hero of me either. The first happened in the spring of my first-form year.

Every student had to participate in some sport each session, and there was ample opportunity for everybody to do so, no matter how poor an athlete he might be. There were not only varsity and junior varsity teams but also house teams, intermediates, and midgets. My age and height qualified me as a midget as far as baseball was concerned; my weight would have ruled me out for midget football or wrestling.

A fellow as slow as I couldn't make the regular team, but I was a good hitter, so I became the midget team's pinch hitter. We didn't have a long season and I hadn't been called upon much, but in our final game against the Peddie midgets, my big chance finally came. In the bottom half of the ninth inning Peddie was ahead by one run, but Lawrenceville had runners on both third and second base. There were two out and a not very good hitter was slated to bat next. "Get in there and pinch-hit" came the command to me from our coach.

I waited out one ball and then connected with a fastball that was right in the groove and drove it out on a line between and past the Peddie right and center fielders. Our man scored with the tying run from third base and our man scored with the winning run from second. Surely I was a hero?

No. Unfortunately a desperate relay from the Peddie center fielder to the Peddie right fielder to the Peddie first baseman nipped me before I could manage to wobble to that base! Three out, the runs didn't count, and Peddie had won the game by one run!

Midget games being of little importance in the frame of the school's athletic life, that experience was more laughable among my contemporaries than it was tragic. I didn't store it up to tell a psychiatrist if I ever had to explain the youthful traumas that affected later life. But a much more serious sports misfortune befell me the following year, even though in this case it was not truly my doing.

Lawrenceville had the best baseball pitcher that season in varsity prep-school circles. He never lost a school game that he pitched, and he virtually never allowed an earned run. The New York Yankees signed him up right after he left Lawrenceville—he was not very bright, as you will see, and he never went on to college—and although he never made the big leagues, he had considerable success for a while with one of their Class AAA minor league farm teams. In any case, he was going to pitch the baseball game against our big rival, the Hill School, and it was a foregone conclusion that the game was in the bag for Lawrenceville.

Two weeks before the game there was a final examination in what was then a compulsory one-term course, Biblical Scripture. I sat next to that pitcher during the test and proceeded to answer the questions as they came up, the first one being "Name the books of the New Testament." When the Bible instructor started to grade the papers that night and came to the pitcher's paper, he found that his answer to that first question read, "Schwed, Matthew, Mark, Luke, John . . ." He had copied my name at the top of my paper before going on to copy the rest!

The pitcher was called up and placed on probation and so did not even dress for the Hill game. We lost. I can't quite see how it was my fault, but I always felt it was—at least sort of.

CHAPTER 13

A Bird in the Hand

The glorious days of badminton

I looked up in some annoyance as an unidentified flying object seemed to descend from the heavens, only to land right in the middle of the salad I had just started eating. The family was having a picnic lunch on the beach, and one of the children had brought along a department-store toy "badminton set" that a doting aunt had sent for Christmas. This was its first time out of the box, and a doubles game of some sort had been organized. I hadn't been paying it much attention for reasons that will shortly become clear, so the bombardment of my salad was as unexpected as it was unwelcome. I gingerly separated the object, which turned out to be a plastic version of a real badminton shuttlecock, or "bird" as it's known in the vernacular, and handed it over to an apologetic Laura, my younger daughter, who had been the one to send it flying in my luncheon's direction.

"Sorry, Dad, and thanks," she said as I returned it to her, "this must bring back old days for you. Badminton was really your game, I've heard tell."

"You've heard right, Laurie," I said a little stiffly, "but no purist could by any stretch of the imagination call what you four are doing badminton. If there's one sport I'm a complete snob about it is badminton, and that's because it truly *was* my game, and I played in championship circles. So I really am somewhat contemptuous of

83

ersatz badminton, such as you're playing, even if it's fun. For one thing, the true game must be played indoors, where there isn't even a breath of wind, and on a level surface where the lines on the court are drawn with meticulous accuracy. They say baseball is a game of inches, which is true, but badminton is every bit as much so. If a tennis court's measurements were off by a little bit it wouldn't matter too much. But if a badminton court's layout had the lines drawn a couple of inches incorrectly it would throw off much of the technique that makes champions. Also, it is vital to have the best equipment, for badminton, although it calls for the power and smashing that tennis does, also constantly requires infinitely deft and subtle strokes that simply can't be executed regularly with anything less than the best racquets and the best birds. You can't play as you are doing on a beach and call it badminton—it's a sacrilege. If you have to call it anything, try 'battledore and shuttle.' That's the ancient game played with paddles from which badminton sprang."

"Oh, come off it, Dad," said Roger, who had been digging into his luncheon undisturbed by extraterrestrial phenomena, "what's so sacred about badminton?"

"Sir," I replied with as much haughtiness as a man can summon when a plastic bird has mixed sand into his salad mayonnaise, "you are speaking of the sport I love! And if you had been taking a young woman dancing at the Rainbow Room in Rockefeller Center in the fall of 1941, instead of waiting around for another seventeen years to be born, you might have been pretty surprised to see what happened when the music was interrupted to allow the floor show to go on. The lights went up and what came out? A chanteuse? A stand-up comedian? A fashion parade? Tap dancers? No.

"The feature of the evening was an exhibition badminton match between two of the game's finest professionals, Ken Davidson and Hugh Forgie, who embellished their usual world-class playing skill with such a repertoire of stunning trick shots as to leave you gasping. The Rainbow Room management knew that this act was a crowd pleaser because these same two athletes had just recently been a sensation as a part of the Radio City Music Hall's stage show. Originally scheduled there as an unusual stunt, it was held over at the Music Hall week after week, even while the jugglers, acrobats, and trained animals moved on across the country to less prestigious vaudeville stops."

Roger doesn't give up too easily. "What was so fascinating about it?" he asked. "It's just another racquet game, isn't it?"

"In a way, yes," I answered, "as far as the strong strokes are concerned. The smashes and the 'clears' over an opponent's head involve the same sort of athletic vigor and power as comparable shots in tennis or squash. It's in the delicate, soft strokes, which are half the game, that badminton differs, and it's essentially in those that top-grade equipment is a necessity. A superior badminton racquet weighs five and a half ounces, and a difference of half an ounce is very considerable. With a weapon that light, good badminton players can fake a hard shot and then suddenly simply waft over a drop shot with a flick of the fingers. A comparable deception in tennis or squash requires the wrist and can't be concealed up to the last moment so subtly and effectively.

"Then there's the matter of a real badminton bird, which is a half sphere of cork topped by a crown of goose feathers. I don't remember anything else in metrology except what a bird must weigh—73.85 grains, or about one-sixth of an ounce—and practically no deviation from that is tolerated in the manufacture of true birds. They *must* be just right for championship levels of play, and besides, they take a tremendous beating in a tough match."

"Why?" asked my older daughter, Kathy, who had been listening in. "If the shots are so soft and delicate, why are the birds damaged so much?"

"There's a fairly equal balance between those sorts of shots and slam-bang stuff," I said, "and a hard smash can produce a velocity in a bird of better than a hundred sixty miles per hour, and at very close quarters. Still, unless you're hit in the eye or something, being hit by a hard smash doesn't hurt more than a smart sting, since one-sixth of an ounce isn't exactly a lethal weapon. But a bird itself takes quite a licking, and good players have to discard one after not too many points have been played. In a close fifteen-point game, the likelihood is that three or four birds will be used. The whole thing is wildly different from what you've been playing on the beach, the only similarity being that you're trying to hit an object back and forth over a high net without allowing it to drop to the ground. I'll admit that it may be fun, but it's about as much like the true sport of badminton as a pony cart is to a racing car."

Greg, who is my elder son, chimed in. "Admittedly, it sounds somewhat more violent than croquet or chess, but does it really compare with tennis, a game we all play energetically, for action and exercise? It sounds as if it's more a battle of wits than of bodies."

"All I can tell you, Greg, is that since it's a game involving deception, you can't anticipate the way you can in other racquet games. You know that even a slow runner can cover the tennis court very well because experience has made him alert to what sort of shot his opponent is likely to make and where it's apt to come. But in badminton, if your opponent is any good you're constantly being double-crossed and having to extend yourself to go for a shot that you would have sworn was much more likely to be hit elsewhere. So it's a game of constant striding and stretching and reversals of direction, and an hour of really competitive singles play can be devastating, even if you're in good condition.

"A badminton court is only about three-fifths the size of a tennis court, so you don't do nearly as much running. Instead, you try to return to midcourt after every shot. You've no idea where you may have to go next, and midcourt is the best common take-off point. A good opponent can conceal what he intends to do right up until the racquet meets the bird, and the result can be anything, from a 'clear' aimed over your head for your extreme backhand corner to a gentle tap that sends the bird barely skimming over the five-foot net, to drop like a plummet near your forehand sideline, no more than a few inches past the net. So badminton players not only work up considerably more sweat than do tennis players, but they also pick up quite a few pulled muscles or ligaments over the course of a season, unless they're lucky."

"How good were you?" Laura asked.

"Pretty good, dear, certainly a lot better than I ever was at any other sport, including tennis. I took up badminton in the late 1930's, when it was a very popular winter sport in the New York City area, for at that time there was virtually no indoor tennis. So badminton was played in armories, schools, and churches. I was fortunate enough to join the Old Sixty-ninth Badminton Club, so named for the armory in which we played. My initial luck was in choosing that place simply because it was close to my office at that time. But the real luck was that in doing so I learned the game from the two best teaching professionals around, the ones I told you about who put on the show at the Music Hall and the Rainbow Room, Ken Davidson and Hugh Forgie. They were such an attraction that the club's membership boasted several players of national-championship calibre. As I progressed I could watch and later actually play with such stars as Billy Markham and Clint Stephens, Metropolitan or Eastern champions, respectively, who threatened to win the Nationals in any year when the incomparable David Freeman of California wasn't playing. It all turned me into a pretty good player fairly quickly. In my first year of competition I won the Metropolitan Class C Championship, and the following year the Class B tournament. That earned me Class A status and an entry into the National championships, which were held that year at the Old Sixty-ninth. My glory was short-lived because I drew David Freeman in the very first round, and Freeman is far and away the greatest badminton player this country ever produced. He is the only American ever to have won the World Championship, being absolutely unbeatable from 1939 to 1942; after the war he returned and reigned again right into the late 1940's. Freeman knocked me off, casually coasting along for our two-game match while I nearly killed myself trying to win a point or two, which is just about what I did and no more. But it's been glory enough to meet old badminton players and be able to say that I played Dave Freeman in the

Nationals. And I did make a headline in the sports section the next day: FREEMAN EASILY DEFEATS NEW YORK PLAYER IN BADMINTON NATIONALS.

My wife, Toni, had a question. "If badminton was so pleasant a game and so many people played it in New York, why did it fade out of sight so completely? I never knew anyone who played the sort of game you're talking about except you, and you played it before we met. The only badminton I know is what you've been so snobbish about, here on the beach."

"I think it was basically because the city armories and the churches had been the principal homes for New York badminton prior to World War Two, but between 1942 and 1945 they were commandeered, the armories for military use and the play spaces in the churches for civilian defense matters. After the war badminton somehow got lost in the shuffle. The armories were converted for indoor tennis, which was popular with a lot of people, while there were not enough old-time badminton enthusiasts and promotors left to resist the change. Old-time players like me knew they were no longer up to top-level singles and willingly turned to the less debilitating game of indoor tennis. Consequently, badminton, like so many of the charms of New York City forty or more years ago—open two-decker buses on Fifth Avenue, and the Hippodrome, for example—faded from view. Badminton is still a very popular sport in other sections of this country, however, particularly in the far West and along the Canadian border. What's more, nearly fifty countries send competitors to the World Championship, an event that draws large and enthusiastic crowds. I went to Wembley Stadium in London a few years ago to see the world's best in action, and the best turned out to be the Indonesians. I understand that they still are, and they certainly were marvelous players, but I'd still risk a modest bet on Dave Freeman if he were still around."

Kathy looked at me curiously. "You continue to like playing tennis so much right up to this day, even though you now invariably stick to doubles and sometimes play with people of a considerably lower level than your normal game. If you liked badminton so much, haven't you ever been tempted to have a go at it again under the same sort of changed conditions?"

I grinned at her. "No, Kathy, I get enough pulled muscles these days running for a bus. Sometimes during spring cleaning Toni finds my old Jack Purcell badminton racquet lying high upon a closet shelf and inquires politely if *now* she can throw it away. I always respond that it's the closest thing I have to a family heirloom, and what's an extra five and a half ounces of junk, considering all the other useless stuff I've crammed onto that shelf? Toni, being the sterling woman she is, sighs, dusts off the racquet, and leaves it there for another year.

"Yet the fact of the matter is that the last time I ever actually used that racquet was around noon on Sunday, December 7, 1941. In the middle of a game a fellow came running out of the office of the badminton club screaming to us all on the floor to come and listen to the radio—Pearl Harbor was being bombed! Two months later I was in the Army and four years later out of it, and badminton vanished as completely from my life as ships that pass in the night.

"At this stage I intend to keep it that way. So thank you for inviting me into this travesty you call badminton, but I prefer to keep my fond memories of the real game intact. I'll just finish what that plastic bird left of this salad and then go swimming."

CHAPTER 14

Losers Weepers?

The triumphs of the defeated

To win is the understandable and admirable goal of any serious sports contestant, but even tough-minded former football coach Vince Lombardi added that winning wasn't everything. Of course his dictum was delivered back in 1962, before the notion of the bottom line had infected so much of American life and professional sports involving huge sums of money had taken over so thoroughly from the old amateur days. Back then sportsmanship and even Arthurian romantic ideals often captured the public's imagination, and every sport has its legends of stars whose major claim to fame, or at least affectionate memory, reposes chiefly in a gallant but losing effort.

Perhaps the outstanding example, because he persevered for so many years, was Sir Thomas Lipton, England's premier yachtsman. He first tried to win the America's Cup in 1899 with *Shamrock I*, tried again in 1901 with *Shamrock II* and yet again in 1903 with *Shamrock III*. Three winning races took the Cup in those days, and the United States boats didn't lose one of the nine races to Sir Thomas. The most gracious of losers, he became beloved by Americans, who not only wanted to see him win a race now and then, but (with the exception of the members of the New York Yacht Club) probably would have been happy to see him actually win the Cup at least once. It didn't happen, but after an interval of

17 years, during which time he sold a lot of Lipton's tea to Americans, he built *Shamrock IV* and returned for his most serious challenge in 1920, when he won two races before succumbing to the United States defender. Encouraged, he made a final try with *Shamrock V* in 1930, the first year in which four victories were required, but this time he won none of them, and he finally called it quits. But Sir Thomas Lipton will be remembered fondly by yachting enthusiasts long after many of them are unable to remember the name of Alan Bond, the man who finally did break the United States' hold on the Cup in 1983 to take it away, even if temporarily, to Australia.

If one were asked who, pound for pound, was the greatest fighter ever, any answer would elicit screams of protest from boxing fans who disagreed. But there is no one who would contest the right of Sugar Ray Robinson to be considered. Robinson was a natural welterweight who won that division's championship in 1946 and defended it successfully until 1951, when he knocked out the middleweight champion, Jake LaMotta, thus becoming a double titleholder. He subsequently relinquished the welterweight title and won the middleweight title four more times, a feat unparalleled in boxing history. Randy Turpin defeated him by a decision in 1951, but two months later Robinson knocked out Turpin to reclaim the title. That made number two. In 1952, after a fight against the light-heavyweight champion, Joey Maxim, which I'll describe a little further on, Robinson announced his retirement from the ring, but in 1955 he returned and knocked out the then middleweight champion, Carl (Bobo) Olsen in the second round, for number three. The following year Gene Fullmer outpointed Robinson, but five months later Robinson once again regained his crown, number four, by knocking out Fullmer. Later that year Carmen Basilio won the title by outpointing Sugar Ray in a split decision, and once again Robinson reversed things by beating Basilio in the return fight, and that made number five.

Robinson fought almost 150 fights in all and was beaten only three times; he subsequently reversed two of those setbacks. Now hear about the third—the one defeat he didn't avenge, which in the minds of most boxing experts was his most glorious fight.

That was when, although outweighed by almost 20 pounds, Robinson made a bid for the light-heavyweight championship held by Joey Maxim. It turned out to be just about the hottest day of the summer of 1952; by evening the thermometer at Yankee Stadium still registered 104°. Under the strong lights above, the air around the fighters battling in the ring was closer to 120°. The fight was scheduled for 15 rounds; in 13 rounds Robinson piled up such a big lead over Maxim that he seemingly couldn't lose. But the heat overcame him, and when he tried to walk out for the fourteenth round, he collapsed. Maxim gained credit for knocking him out in that round. After that fight Robinson announced his retirement, but as you know, he came out of retirement three years later to reclaim the middleweight laurels three more times. His winning record was fabulous—truly unmatched—but Robinson's crowning achievement was to have stepped so far out of his weight class and come so close to winning, only to succumb to the blast furnace of a sweltering New York night. That losing fight was really the epic moment in Robinson's career.

What does any veteran follower of tennis remember about Baron Gottfried von Cramm? Not any of his many great victories, both in Europe and in the United States in an era in which he successfully battled an incredible number of superstars, but rather the defeat that made him truly famous in tennis annals. It came in the interzone finals of the 1937 Davis Cup, fought between his country, Germany, and the United States.

The holder of the Davis Cup was England, but that country had lost the star who had been responsible for the victory the previous year, Fred Perry, because he had turned professional. So England, the defending champion, had a comparatively weak team, and it was a foregone conclusion that the winner of the interzone final the United States or Germany, would beat England in the final, and take the Davis Cup. The United States was a distinct favorite, for the greatest player in the world at that time, Donald Budge, was on the U.S. team, and one such outstanding star almost invariably assures a winning team: he will win his two singles matches and will team up with a partner to win the doubles, making the three wins necessary for one nation to win a Davis Cup match against another.

In the interzone final Budge did indeed win his first encounter against the German Henner Henkel, but von Cramm unexpectedly beat the other American singles player, Bitsy Grant. The next day Budge and his partner, Gene Mako, won the doubles match, so things seemed to look rosy for the United States team. Grant was favored to beat Henkel, which would end things and make the fifth match, between Budge and von Cramm, meaningless. But Henkel pulled an upset and beat Grant, which meant that the fifth match would be decisive that year. Well . . . not to worry. No one was going to beat Don Budge. Certainly not von Cramm, who had been beaten by Budge in straight sets in both the Queen's Club and Wimbledon tournaments only weeks before.

Many people consider their contest the most outstanding tennis match ever played. They both played superlatively, with von Cramm coming from behind to win the first set 8–6, and then after being behind 40–love, breaking Budge's serve in the twelfth game of the second set to win the set 7–5. Budge took the third set 6–4 and, after the rest period, won the fourth set as well, 6–2, to tie the match. Von Cramm, whose record of winning critical fifth sets was unmatched, darted ahead to 4–1. But Budge held his serve and broke von Cramm's to reach 4–4. That's when the match started in earnest, the crowd divided equally in favoring the two men, and it seemed tragic that one must eventually lose. At 7–6, with Budge serving, the game went to deuce six times; Budge had five match points when, off balance and with von Cramm seemingly in control of the point at net, he made a desperation shot that flashed down the sideline just out of the German's reach and bit the corner of the court. Budge was victorious. Had the shot been six inches longer, or six inches more to the right, the score would have been back to deuce once again, and the match might have gone on until one of the players dropped.

Budge's fame doesn't rest upon his victory in that spectacular match, even though it certainly is one of the highlights of his brilliant career. As for von Cramm, if that match had never taken place, I doubt that anyone would name him among the top two or three dozen greatest tennis players of all time, or even recall him when exchanging stories about the many outstanding players of that era—even though he was a splendid tennis player with many notable performances to his credit. His gallant loss to Don Budge is unquestionably the only reason why he will always be considered among the game's immortals.

If Bill Bradley hadn't decided to squeeze in a few years of professional basketball, after being a Rhodes scholar at Oxford, before embarking on his political career, it would have been too bad, for he became an indispensable cog in the greatest New York Knick team in memory, the championship outfit of the early 1970's. Even if he had not turned professional at all, he would still be remembered as a legendary hero for his part in a game that his college team, Princeton, lost.

In Bradley's senior year, 1964–65, Princeton was invited to play in the Christmas Festival tournament at Madison Square Garden, and was drawn to face the then top-ranked college basketball team in the country, Michigan. Princeton had a good team, primarily because they had Bradley, but hardly anyone thought they had a chance of making much more than a fairly respectable showing against the giants from the Midwest. They were thought to have no chance at all of winning.

But Bradley dominated the Michigan five almost single-handedly and played them into the floor. He made every sort of shot, faked Michigan defenders out of their shoes, stole balls, fed teammates with unbelievable passes, and on defense held his own man to one point. He himself scored 41 points, and when he sat down on the bench some four and a half minutes before the end of the game, the entire Garden crowd rose to its feet and screamed and applauded him for a full three minutes, the most clamorous ovation ever given to a basketball player, college or professional, in that arena.

The reason Bill Bradley went to the bench with still more than four minutes to go was because he had made the mistake of defending against his man too closely, when it wasn't necessary, and he had fouled out—his fifth personal foul. Two of his starting-five teammates had also done so, and without those three— Bradley in particular—Michigan, which was by then 12 points behind and apparently solidly beaten, rolled all over the Princeton substitutes and finally pulled out the game, winning by one basket, turning the game into a catastrophe for Bradley, for he was such a solid team man. It was his performance in that game more than any other that caused him to be voted the outstanding college basketball player of the year, won him the Sullivan Award as the best amateur athlete of the year, and made him the first-choice selection of the New York Knickerbockers in the annual player draft, despite their knowledge that Bradley, about to go off to Oxford on his Rhodes scholarship, might never choose to play professional basketball. They couldn't afford to lose such a gem in case he did decide to play pro ball, and it turned out they made a wise decision. Of course, Bradley's fame both at Princeton and with the Knicks is based upon many other great shows he put on—winning ones—but that gallant if losing performance against Michigan on December 30, 1964, was the stuff around which heroic sagas are written.

Golf gives us a classic example of an athlete's achieving far greater fame as a loser than he ever did as a winner. In 1968 the Argentinian golfer, Roberto de Vicenzo, competing in the Masters tournament at Augusta, Georgia, was battling with Bob Goalby for the lead as each, playing with different partners for the round, were approaching the last holes of the fourth and final round. De

Vicenzo, partnered by Tommy Aaron, had a birdie 3 on the 17th and next-to-last hole, but Aaron, who was keeping de Vicenzo's scorecard while de Vicenzo kept his (which is the rule for such tournaments), made a mistake and entered Roberto's score on the 17th as a 4. They then played the final hole, the 18th, on which de Vicenzo missed an eight-foot putt for his par 4, and scored a bogie 5. He was probably upset by this misadventure as he went to the scorer's tent to check the card that Aaron had turned in for him, and didn't notice that Aaron had penciled in a 4 instead of the 3 he had scored on the 17th, even though Aaron had the total score for the round right—65. But with that 4 on the card, the total added up to 66, and under the unrelenting rules of golf de Vicenzo's card had to have the total changed to a 66, which was just enough to enable Bob Goalby to win the tournament over de Vicenzo by one stroke!

The most gracious of losers, de Vicenzo kept a brave face on things afterward, didn't blame Aaron at all, and told reporters, "I am just a stupid." But that incident, which one would have thought carried nothing but heartbreak for Roberto, actually made him a giant golf figure in the United States. Up to that time he had been known as a fine golfer almost exclusively in his own country and in England. The British love foreign golfers who keep coming over for the British Open year after year, and de Vicenzo had finished well up several times before he came through and finally won the event in 1967. That had made him an idol in England, but in the United States he was a virtual unknown until this 1968 Masters. Had he won it, he would, of course, have established a reputation over here, but probably not as enduring a one as he did by losing as a result of a freak occurrence. As a case in point, de Vicenzo's name carries much more weight in golf's history than that of Bob Goalby or, for that matter, of Tommy Aaron, who won the Masters in 1973.

A loser in an individual sport has a better chance of shrugging off or even deriving satisfaction from a game in which he played well but lost, than does an athlete who, through tough luck, loses a vital game for his team. Two baseball players who come to mind in this connection are Fred Merkle of the 1908 New York Giants and Ralph Branca of the 1951 Brooklyn Dodgers. Merkle's "boner" was certainly understandable, and although it has been assigned the blame for losing the pennant for the Giants, I like to think that he got more sympathy than harsh criticism in later years, after the first passions of disappointed Giant rooters had died down. In the ninth inning of the crucial game against the Chicago Cubs that would decide the National league championship, Merkle was on first base and a teammate was on third with the score tied and two out. The Giant at bat made a hit, and Merkle, seeing the runner score from third with what should have been the game clincher and the crowd pour out onto the field, turned and made for the club-house without going on to second. Johnny Evers, the Cubs' second baseman, got his hands on the ball—whether what he ended up with was *the* ball or not never was proved—and stepped on second base for the forceout that ended the inning and negated the apparent winning run. So the score was still 1–1, and further play was impossible because the crowd had taken over the field. It was ruled that a playoff would be held the day after the regular season ended if it turned out to be necessary, and it did. The Giants and the Cubs wound up in a tie, and the Cubs won the playoff 4–2. So Merkle's famous "boner" cost the Giants the pennant, if you want to look at it that way. It surely wasn't the *only* thing that cost the pennant, but it's the one that's been immortalized. With it, however, Fred Merkle has been immortalized, too, instead of being completely forgotten as he would have been otherwise. I can't think his mental error, a small one under normal circumstances, was unforgivable, and the unique aspect of the occurrence has made it a kind of comic high point in baseball history for everybody except rabid 1908 Giant rooters.

As for Ralph Branca, he was simply unlucky in 1951. He was one of Brooklyn Dodger fans' heroes throughout the season, and a consistent twenty-game winner. The third and decisive game of the playoff against the New York Giants for the National League pennant probably shouldn't have been his to win or lose. It was Don Newcombe's turn to start, and the way Newcombe had been pitching, it was his game to finish too. In the previous three games, Newcombe had gone twenty-one innings without a run being scored against him, and the Dodgers were leading 1–0. Then, in the seventh inning, the Giants squeezed out a run on a sacrifice fly to tie the game. But it didn't seem to matter, for the Dodgers came back in the eighth inning to score three more runs and to take the lead 4–1. The Giants had only one chance left in the bottom of the ninth. One chance? Hardly any chance at all with Newcombe pitching the way he was.

The Giants did put together a couple of scratch singles, however, and then, after Newcombe retired a man on a pop-up, Whitey Lockman drove a second Giant run home. The Dodgers were still ahead 4–2 with one man out, but the Giants had two men on base. Was this the moment for manager Charley Dressen to call in a relief pitcher to finish things off? Newcombe still looked as strong as ever and was burning the ball in, but Dressen decided it was time to call upon his other pitching ace, Branca, and gave the signal that he should come in and pitch to the next Giant batter, Bobby Thomson. Branca threw one pitch for a called strike, and then tried for another. The next moment Thomson had laid on the ball and hit it out of the park, the Giants had won the game 5–4 and the pennant along with it, and Brooklyn was the saddest town in baseball history, including Mudville when the mighty Casey struck out.

But what about Ralph Branca and his emotions at such a loss? At the moment he must have suffered despair, but for him as for others, the passage of years has blunted the tragedy of the moment and enhanced the legend. Baseball fans know that Branca was an exceptionally good pitcher, but exceptionally good pitchers come and go and are barely remembered. Ralph Branca and his connection with Bobby Thomson's "homer that was heard around the world" appear prominently in every baseball history ever written, and the fact that it was Ralph Branca, making only two pitches in the entire game, who delivered the one that Thomson hit, was just tough luck. The number on Branca's uniform was 13, but was it such bad luck after all? Certainly Branca must have been kidded to death often, but, I suspect, with rueful admiration and affection, for he was a splendid pitcher who just happened to have this unforgettable piece of misfortune happen to him—and make him immortal.

The classic case in football of an individual's losing an important game owing to an unfortunate mishap is that of Roy (Wrong Way) Riegels, who played center for the University of California in the 1929 Rose Bowl contest against Georgia Tech. He picked up a Georgia Tech fumble and in the excitement of doing so and probably never before having had the opportunity to carry the ball, ran frantically toward the *wrong* goal line! That led directly to a Georgia Tech safety that won the game for the southern team 8–7. It's a sad story without much comfort or moral to it, although it certainly gave Riegels an extraordinary amount of publicity then and later and a nickname, "Wrong Way," that was his and his alone until Douglas Corrigan flew the Atlantic to Europe and claimed he meant to fly westward across the continent.

Owen Johnson's *Stover at Yale* was a very famous college novel published in the early part of this century, when, admittedly, sports were more romantic than they are now. An important football game is one of the plot elements. Dink Stover comes up to Yale from his prep school, Lawrenceville, where he has been All-American Scholastic end on the football team. He plays end because he doesn't weigh enough to be a back in that crunching-power era of American football, but he is a lambent flame on the football field and the best athlete Yale has. In the preparations for Yale's big game of the year, against Princeton, the coach draws Stover aside and explains that he's got to put Stover into the backfield and play him throughout the game, both on offense and defense, even though he knows it will destroy Stover's opportunity to star at end and be an All-American. If he doesn't do so, Yale will be murdered by this much heavier championship Princeton team. At least Stover is fast and may get away for some runs that no other back on the Yale team is capable of. Stover, although an extremely mediocre punter, is the best Yale has, and kicking will be very important in this game. In any case, the coach explains, although he knows he is asking Stover to make a tremendous sacrifice, it is for Dear Old Yale. Of course, we all know what Stover does. He puts aside thoughts of personal glory and starts to try to make his punts carry higher and farther.

But Stover's efforts are to no avail. He does the best he can, but the Yale team is so outmanned that it is no contest. When Yale has the ball they are unable to make a first down, and Stover has to punt time and time again. The best he can do is to try to punt low and away from the receiver, and hope to get a roll. If he can manage to move the ball downfield some 30 yards or so, he's doing well. But on the one or two occasions when Princeton punts, the kicks spiral high and deep, 50 yards or more, and Stover, playing safety as well as every other position he can, is immediately buried under an avalanche of Princeton tacklers. At halftime Princeton leads by 18–0, which in the days before the forward pass, is comparable to a halftime score today of 35–0.

The dispirited and weary Yale team drags itself to the dressing room at the half. The coach makes no attempt to correct technical mistakes or suggest new strategems, but simply tells them, "You're up against a great Princeton team, the greatest I can remember. You can't win. You never had a chance to win. But Yale, you're going to do something to make us proud of you. You're going to hold that score where it is! You're going to die game, every mother's son of you! And when the game is over we're going to be prouder of your second half that the whole blooming Princeton bunch. That's your chance. Make us rise up and yell for you!"

And the Yale team does just that, though driven back to the brink of their own goal line more than once. They dig in furiously in a pair of last-ditch defenses and stop Princeton from scoring another touchdown. It is the last minutes of play, and now Stover knows he has enough stamina to last out the game. He decides to shoot the works and for the first time really leads the team into an embattled offense. The team catches maniacal fire and marches down the field to within yards of the Princeton goal, but as they line up for the next play, which may score a touchdown, the whistle blows, signifying the end of the game. Stover is frantic.

" 'Mr. Referee, it can't be time! Mr. Referee—'

" 'Game's over,' said Captain Dana's still voice. 'Get together, Yale. A cheer for Princeton, now. Make it a good one!' " And they give the cheer.

Stover's disappointment has been too severe. As he slumps his way back to the gymnasium, the score goes over and over in his mind. " 'Eighteen to nothing—to nothing! It should have been eighteen to six. Eighteen to nothing! It's awful—awful! If I could only punt!' "

But then in the dressing room the coach talks to the team again.

" 'A great Princeton team licked you—licked you well. That's all. You deserved to score. You didn't. Hard luck. But those who saw you try for it won't forget it. All Yale is proud of that second half. So no talk about what might have been—grin and take your medicine.' "

The chapter ends with Stover going out, head erect, back to meet his college, no longer shrinking from the ordeal, proud of his captain, proud of his coach, and proud of a lesson he has learned that means more than a victory.

Now I admit that modern readers probably find the episode from *Stover at Yale* so corny as to be nauseating. Perhaps if I were to read it for the first time today, I'd have a similar reaction myself, but I read it when I was a schoolboy more than half a century ago, in a more romantic era, and I thought it touching and admirable. In any event, while it is, admittedly, fiction, not fact like my other stories, it belongs in this review of sports losers who were, perhaps, really winners.

I have saved the happiest story about a triumphant loser for the end. It is about track star Harrison Dillard, hurdler extraordinaire, who completely dominated the high hurdles events, both indoor and outdoor, in the decade from 1946 to 1955. He simply never lost, and he held the world's record and was at his peak in the 110-meter hurdle event in 1948, which was the year the Olympic Games were to be held in London.

Now the United States picks its Olympic contestants for the track and field team differently than other nations, who simply decide on the basis of past and current performances who can best represent them. The United States doesn't leave it up to judgment or opinion at all. A full-scale Olympic-tryouts meet is held a few weeks prior to the Olympics, and the first three finishers in each event become our Olympic team, regardless of what has gone before or who has established him or herself as the best in an event. This eliminates any personal bias or favoritism, which is a good thing, but it also sometimes precipitates a disaster, and none has ever seemed more disastrous than what happened to Harrison Dillard in the 110-meter hurdle event in the Olympic tryouts in 1948.

Dillard had been unbeaten in the event for some three years, but for the first and I believe only time in his long career, his foot caught the top bar of a hurdle somewhere along the course, and he fell flat on the track! Naturally he did not place among the first three, so it seemed that Dillard's almost certain expectations of making the Olympic team and winning a gold medal had gone down the drain.

He thought it over, and since the trials for the 100-meter dash had not been held yet, he decided to enter that event and see what he could do. Dillard had never competed in the dash, but a world-class hurdler has to be a fine sprinter, and Dillard thought he might possibly squeeze into third place in the tryouts and at least make the team. That is exactly what happened: he placed third and was named to the team. The real payoff, however, came a few weeks later in London. By that time Dillard had polished up his sprinting style, and to everyone's amazement he won the 100-meter dash, not only beating his two fellow Americans but also all of the world's best from foreign nations.

That most satisfying happy ending would wind up the Harrison Dillard story, one might think. But no. The high hurdles was the event that belonged to Dillard, and he wasn't going to allow any usurper who by sheer chance had happened to win the 1948 Olympic title to take it away from him. He never competed seriously in the dash again, but resumed his unchecked domination of the hurdles event, and in the next Olympics, the 1952 Games held at Helsinki, he breezed off and took the gold medal in record time.

Harrison Dillard was one loser who didn't weep for long.

CHAPTER 15

Oh, to Be in England!

A tennis player's problems across the Atlantic

There wasn't much point in it, but I leaned out of the window of our London hotel room and peered up at the sky. I had already packed my gear and my racquet in my tennis bag in preparation for keeping a date to play at a club to which I had been invited. The sky was a solid gray and there had been a sprinkle of light rain a while back. The morning paper lay on the breakfast table and the weather prediction read, "Intermittent showers with bright patches."

Still, I was sanguine. This wasn't my first trip to England by a long shot; I had caught on to English weather while spending a year in Devon prior to D day, and I had had my observations confirmed in annual visits I had taken to London in subsequent years to look for British books my firm might want to publish in the United States. I had found that half the time the weather prediction there is "Showers with bright patches," and in the other half it's "Sunny intervals with occasional showers." They flip a coin at the weather bureau to decide which one they'll use on that particular day, and since they both mean the same thing, it doesn't matter which side of the coin comes up. Even more to the point: both predictions are almost always absolutely correct. You practically never get a day of steady rain, and very seldom a day of uninterrupted sunny weather. So I learned that it doth not profit a man to be particularly cheerful if he awakes to a beautiful clear morning on a day when he's scheduled to play tennis, nor should he be downcast if it's raining. The chances are that the game will be played, especially if it's scheduled for a shale court. This is highly likely because shale is a very popular surface for courts in England, and with good reason.

Shale courts do not exist in any numbers in the United States, but they make great sense in England. Shale is a fine-grained, thinly bedded rock that splits easily into smooth layers. Small pieces are fitted together like a mosaic, but with enough space between pieces to permit water to seep through and drain off below. It makes a very acceptable tennis surface, with the great advantage that one can play on it almost the minute the rain stops.

So no matter what the weather is when you're ready to start off for your game, you don't hesitate, or worry about it, or call your opponent to see how he feels about things. You just pick up your things and go. If it's raining when you get there, you simply dress and wait for the rain to stop. That's usually in no more than about 10 minutes, possibly less. Then you start playing, and it may well be that after 20 minutes or so a slight drizzle starts again, but the rain practically never pelts down hard the way it can in the U.S. Shakespeare, accustomed to British weather, wrote: "It falleth like the gentle rain from Heaven." Since shale courts are not at all slippery, and since most of us have nylon stringing in our racquets these days, you just keep on playing for a while.

But let's say that the light rain has continued falling so steadily that five minutes later you're actually getting uncomfortably wet. You quit and make for shelter, but chances are that after another five minutes the rain will have stopped again and you'll be apt to enjoy a long enough "sunny interval" to finish your match. It's true that the English Slazenger balls, which are somewhat heavier to start with than American-made balls, can get so soggy that you feel you are stroking a shot put, but what's fair for one player is fair for another. The best idea is simply to aim to clear the net by a really safe margin and whack each shot with everything you've got. It's a different game, but it's sort of fun. Of course, if you're really a profligate type, you might be inclined to open another can of balls.

I happened to know that the game in which I'd been invited to play that day at London's prettiest club, Hurlingham, was to be on shale, so conditions didn't worry me as much as they might have had we been scheduled to play on another type of court. My invitation was for two o'clock; we'd probably get enough rain before then to make grass impossible and Hard-Tru unpleasant, but shale would be all right. Personally, I always prefer to play in the morning, but the British don't seem to think that's legal. They always seem to schedule reservations for the afternoon. I suspect it's the Englishman's almost sacred respect for luncheon that dictates this. He doesn't want to play really early, and even less does he want to cut into luncheon time, so he doesn't plan to start any game until he'll have had a chance to tuck away a steak-and-kidney pie and a sweet. Well, at least that leaves early-bird Americans like me the mornings for visiting museums and art galleries.

I may sound a little bitter, but please understand that there are many things about tennis in England that I like very much. Balls come in a set of four, rather than three, which is extremely nice, even if somewhat expensive. A steady supply of tea is invariably ready to be poured, and, believe it or not, if one can put aside one's youthful American prejudices briefly, one may well find it a better restorative after a tough match than Coke or Gatorade. The same can be said when you go to the locker room of a fine British club, like Wimbledon or Queens, and find a row of very long, very deep bathtubs, each in a private cubicle with water of exactly the right temperature run by the attendant. There was a time when an English tennis club had a single, rather poor shower head, obviously installed for Americans and other strange types who insisted upon showering, but times have changed and there are plenty of decent showers around nowadays. I know most Americans prefer a shower to a bath any day and so do many younger British players, and so did I once, but the fact is that there's nothing like luxuriating a while in one of those marvelously roomy tubs, in very hot water, after a couple of tough sets. At least there's nothing like it at my present age.

Another big plus in the British way of tennis is that at several of the best clubs, court reservations are for an hour and a quarter, rather than the more usual one-hour session. That extra 15 minutes makes all the difference if you're limited to a single reservation. You can have a decent warm-up and still get in a full couple of sets as a rule.

An American can be unnerved by British tribal customs regarding the use of signals on a tennis court. Over there the signal that a ball is out consists of stretching both arms far out to the side, palms down, like a baseball umpire's call of "Safe!" It's the gesture used by American tennis players to indicate that a ball is good. Conversely, if a ball has indeed struck safely within the court lines, the Britisher conveys that fact by jerking his thumb sharply up into the air above his shoulder, which is the motion a baseball umpire, or an American tennis player, uses to make an "Out!" call. This complete reversal of signals can cause consternation in an American visitor. It is, as the farmer said of the big city, amusin' but confusin'. The reason for the mix-up is that the English signals are based on a cricket umpire's gestures, while the American ones copy a baseball umpire's, as originally prescribed and followed for many decades. (These days baseball umpires have become so theatrical that they nearly turn cartwheels while making a simple call.) To be fair, a Britisher will on occasion indicate that a ball is good by extending one hand palm down and moving it gently up and down as if he were patting the head of a large and possibly unfriendly dog. This motion would indeed be recognized by an American to mean "safe," but as it is the lone example of agreement on signals, it only compounds previous confusion.

I do have one strong complaint that is quite apart from tennis, though it does affect my tennis; it concerns the English reticence in the use of first names. Since I've retired from book publishing and no longer make an annual scouting trip, I only return to England every few years. On my last trip, I might not have been able to work up a game at all if I hadn't been able to get in touch with an English author whom I had published in the United States, and who I knew was a keen tennis player. I happened to know who his English publisher was, and was able to reach him through that office. Otherwise I'd have been in bad shape, for in England recalling a name does you very little good unless you also recall an address. If my author's name had been an unusually weird one I suppose I'd have been able to locate him in the telephone directory without knowing his address. But his last name, like those of so many Britishers, was quite a common one; let's say his name was Terrence Foster. If you try to find such a name in the London directory you'll be faced with columns of "Foster, T.," and that will be it. There will be virtually no first names listed, and certainly no Terrence. I never would have found him had I not thought of seeking help from his publisher, and I might have had to walk down Piccadilly with a sign reading TENNIS, ANYONE?

The English are invariably slow, by our standards, about becoming too familiar and using first names early in an acquaintanceship. Fair enough, I say, even if it seems somewhat cool to us, but what is this prejudice about using first names *at all,* even in a functional tool like the telephone directory? It also extends to newspaper summaries of important sporting events. One year I was in London while the French Open was taking place. There was no newspaper coverage of the early rounds except the brief summaries of the results. When I looked at the fine print one morning, I actually experienced a couple of seconds of double-take before I realized that "Mrs. J. M. Lloyd," who had coasted through her first-round match, was indeed none other than our own beloved Chris, whose book I was on the eve of publishing. I suppose it doesn't matter too much on the sports page, but it's infuriating if you're trying to look somebody up in the telephone book!

CHAPTER 16

Many Miles to Go

Bill Bonthron, Glenn Cunningham, and Jack Lovelock

Jack Lovelock was a New Zealander who went to Oxford and who, in 1933, was already known to be one of the world's best mile runners. He had run for Great Britain in the 1932 Olympics the previous year and had also broken the world record for three quarters of a mile. Although still an Oxford undergraduate, he was already a prime candidate to win the 1,500-meter run in the 1936 Olympics three years later.

Bill Bonthron was a junior at Princeton who had never run as an individual in world-class competition. Princeton's track philosophy was that team success was more important than individual achievement, and Bonthron had run a series of astonishingly brilliant anchor legs for Princeton relay teams through the winter season. He had only emerged as a recognized star himself that spring, and then simply because he won so many races so convincingly. On two occasions he had doubled up in a meet to win both the 800-meter and the 1,500-meter runs, first in the dual meet against Harvard, and then in the Intercollegiates. In the dual meet against Yale he had actually pulled off a triple in one afternoon, winning the 3,000-meter run as well as the other two. It was clear that Bonthron was a wonder at the collegiate level, but he had never been up against an internationalist of Lovelock's stature.

Now such an encounter was about to take place. A dual meet pitting the combined teams of Oxford and Cambridge against the combined teams of Princeton and Cornell was scheduled, and Lovelock and Bonthron were slated to meet each other in the mile. Still, despite considerable interest among knowledgeable track and field followers at that time, the meet didn't attract more than about 2,500 spectators to Princeton's Palmer Stadium that day, the majority of them from the college community. I was there as an official on one of the field events, but when the whistle blew calling the two runners to the starting line of the mile run, everyone, including me, stopped whatever they were doing to watch.

I had been very active in track matters in the years just preceding, having served as manager of track and cross-country both in prep school at Lawrenceville and at Princeton, under coach Matty Geis. Matty knew I was an experienced official with a keen interest in Bonthron, whose teams I had managed when he was a freshman and a sophomore. Matty had seen to it that I had a minor job on the field for this meet, so that I could be close to the action. He was aware that Bonthron had no bigger fan than I. Our friendship had continued after I left college, and I invariably saw him when I came back, often bedding down on a couch in his dormitory room if I stayed over for a night. I saw every race he ever ran from the time he entered Princeton, most of them in person. If that wasn't practical, I always made a point of seeing them afterward on the films that were taken, initially by college photographers, and later, when the era of the great milers was in full swing (and that began with this race), by newsreel photographers. This was before television, of course, and such intense interest was generated by a succession of mile-run encounters, that each was covered by the newsreel companies and shown in movie theaters.

This particular race certainly turned out to be the greatest mile ever contested up to that time. Lovelock overtook Bonthron in the stretch and won the race while setting a new world record of 4:07.6. Bonthron's second-place time of 4:08.7 also broke the former world record and set a new American one. Since this was a dual meet, where points counted for a team's success, a little over an hour later Bonthron came back to the track and won the 880-yard run in sparkling time to help the Princeton-Cornell team win the meet. Lovelock was quoted as saying that he considered Bonthron's double that day superior to his own world-record performance.

That was a typically generous and sportsmanlike statement by Lovelock, and it was comforting for a disappointed Bonthron fan like me to hear. But Lovelock proved himself the better miler that day, and did it again later. After all, in 1933 Bonthron was only 20 years old, while Lovelock was 23 and a much more seasoned campaigner.

A year later, however, Bonthron had picked up much more experience as a result of a series of mile and 1,500-meter encounters, both indoors in the winter and outdoors in the spring, against Glenn Cunningham, the acknowledged king of American milers. They had met five times, and Bonthron had won three of the races including the final two. In the last of these he had set a new world record for the 1,500-meter run, which was the equivalent of a 4:05 mile. Meanwhile Lovelock had been running races intermittently in Europe, none particularly spectacular, nor were they important events. Throughout 1934 international interest in the mile had been focused on the United States and the Cunningham-Bonthron rivalry, and for the time being Lovelock was almost forgotten.

The excitement in this country peaked in June 1934, Cunningham and Bonthron's first outdoor meeting. Each had beaten the other once during the indoor season, both times by inches. This spring encounter was going to be the feature of a meet that the Princeton Athletic Association dreamed up as a special treat for commencement weekend. It was called the Princeton Invitation Track Meet, and only a limited number of events were planned and athletes invited, so that only the most appealing events and the world's best athletes would compete. There would be no trial heats, that being unnecessary with the limitation on the number of entries in any event, so the entire meet could take place in an hour's time

in the late afternoon, at the conclusion of the festive alumni
parade. There were no reserved seats and no advance sale of
tickets, which cost one dollar. Anyway, Palmer Stadium could seat
almost 50,000 people, and attendance at track meets invariably
was low, so why would anything more elaborate be necessary?
Princeton knew the Princeton people were excited, but how many
others were likely to be?

The amazing answer is that 50,000 people poured into Princeton on the Pennsylvania Railroad and in cars and buses, and
latecomers had to sit in the aisles or stand behind the back,
uppermost row. The meet itself turned out to be even better than its
billing, and records were set in absolutely every event, including
two world records, Ben Eastman's in the 880, and Glenn Cunningham's in the mile. All the events were wildly exciting and were
won by an eyelash—with one exception. Cunningham's 4:06.7 in
the mile was a walkaway. Bonthron was left far back, finishing
some 40 yards behind the flying Kansan.

There was much dejected discussion among Bonny's rooters
later. Perhaps the buildup had been too great; perhaps the importance of Bill's graduation that same week had increased the pressure on him; perhaps he had made a mistake in playing nine holes
of golf that morning; perhaps he shouldn't have eaten his almost
invariable summer lunch of a pint of vanilla ice cream. The
Bonthron fan club didn't cheer up until a couple of weeks later,
when Bonny beat Cunningham in the NCAA mile by six yards and
set a new NCAA record in so doing. Then, one week after that, he
defeated Cunningham again by a stride in the AAU 1,500-meter
run, setting a new world record for that event. That gave Bonthron
a three-to-two edge over Cunningham in the five races they ran
against each other in 1934, and that year Bonthron was voted
the Sullivan Award trophy as the country's outstanding amateur
athlete.

All of that made his defeat in the Princeton Invitation a memory
best forgotten, but the meet itself certainly wasn't. It had been a
sensational success, and right after it was over plans were afoot to

put it on again the following June and, very likely, make it an annual fixture during commencement week.

But meanwhile, where was Jack Lovelock? He had been unable to accept the Princeton Invitation bid, but fortunately the return dual meet between the combined Oxford-Cambridge and Princeton-Cornell teams was scheduled to be held in London that summer of 1934, and Lovelock and Bonthron would be meeting each other again in the mile. Bonthron seemed to be at his peak, having established his edge over Cunningham, while Lovelock had hardly been heard from for a year. The time differential between London and New York meant that the radio broadcast of the event—no television then, of course—would come in midmorning for me.

I was working at my first job, for a very strict business organization; at that time jobs were so scarce that you grasped at anything, no matter how poor the salary or how restrictive the office regulations. It was among the worst years of the Depression. People punched time clocks, didn't take one minute more for lunch than allowed, worked half a day Saturdays, and nobody had ever heard of anything called a coffee break.

There was a radio shop a couple of blocks away from the office, and I knew that the people there would be listening, for there was enormous interest in this race. I simply had to be in on the radio broadcast. I knew I would never get away with playing hooky from work, so I finally admitted to my immediate boss how much this perhaps silly race meant to me, but so did my job. Could he possibly cover up for me in some fashion for a half an hour or so? It wasn't within his authority just to let me go, but he said he'd mutter something or other about my breaking my eyeglasses and having to go to an optician for repairs. He was a noble gentleman even though he didn't know anything about Lovelock and Bonthron, and cared less.

Along about 10 o'clock, there I was in the radio shop listening to the British broadcaster whipping up anticipation for this first encounter of Lovelock and Bonthron since, as it was indeed then known, "the greatest mile race ever run." It didn't turn out to be quite that again, for the time was slower, but Lovelock beat Bonny once more by a stride. A few weeks later, in Amsterdam, he did it again, but then Bonthron, in what he said would probably be his last race, finally turned the tables and triumphed over Lovelock handily, in Paris. Bill came back to the United States right afterward and went to work with the accounting firm where he stayed all his life. Both Lovelock and Cunningham continued to compete throughout the rest of 1934 and into 1935, setting their sights on 1936 and the upcoming Berlin Olympics. In the end, Bonny hung up his spikes, went out of training, got married, and settled down in a pleasant house in Princeton, commuting to work in New York.

I visited him there early in 1935, and he was wrestling with a problem. The university had received such plaudits for the first Invitation Meet that plans were well under way for a second one in June. Once again the mile was to be the feature event, particularly because this time Jack Lovelock had accepted the invitation to come over and compete against Glenn Cunningham and Gene Venzke, the other top-notch American mile runner. All of them had their eyes on the 1936 Olympic Games, but Bonthron had quit track completely more than half a year ago, and really had no heart to start rigorous training again for what might well be a futile effort to get back on competitive terms with his rivals. The problem was that Princeton desperately wanted Bill to be in the race, not only because his presence would mean that every one of the worlds' best milers would be competing, but especially because this was a sentimental Princeton affair, held in conjunction with commencement and alumni reunions, and Bonthron was the Princeton athletic hero of the era. The university's feelings carried a lot of weight with Bonny, who was so devoted to Princeton that he chose to spend his life there after graduation, but he truly did not want to take up strenuous competitive running again, and he told me so.

One of his reasons was that he had never actually enjoyed running very much in the first place. He did it because it was clear from his schoolboy days at Exeter that he was good at it, and when you get to college you're likely to continue with the sport at which you can make a reputation for yourself. The sport that Bonny truly cared for was golf, and he seized every chance to get out on the course, not only during his undergraduate years but throughout his life. He scored a hole-in-one on the Princeton course just a few weeks before his death in 1983 at the age of 70.

Anyway, after quite a long soliloquy about the conflicting issues in his mind, he said to me, "I'm going to do it! I owe it to Princeton, certainly, and maybe even to myself to see if I can give it this one last try. I suppose, if it works, I can't completely put the idea out of my mind about keeping going for still another year and trying to make it to Berlin, but that's not even worth thinking about now. What I want to concentrate upon now is to get back in shape for the Princeton meet, and that's all."

The promotional buildup for this second Invitation Meet was even bigger than it had been the previous year, for in this meet the three premier milers in the world would all be competing against each other for the first time—it turned out to be the only time as well. The sportswriters dubbed it "the mile of the century"—an encomium they've used several times since for mile races. But this was the first. Once again 50,000 people jammed the stadium and saw a meet as thrilling as the previous year's. In the mile Jack Lovelock maintained the edge he had established over both his rivals in the course of their racing history and won fairly handily. Bonthron made a good enough comeback to beat Cunningham out for second place, but this race demonstrated, at least to me, that Lovelock was the best of them all. It was hard for me to admit, since I was such a Bonthron fan, but he was. A year later, in the 1936 Berlin Olympics, when Bonny had really retired, Lovelock once again nosed out Cunningham in the 1,500-meter run and set a new world record, breaking Bonthron's old 1934 record by one second.

A couple of years later, in 1938, Princeton's reputation in track was still very high as a direct result of Bonthron's prowess and the unique Invitation Meet. Schoolboy stars who previously might never have thought of Princeton as a potential showcase for their talents started to apply for admittance, and Matty Geis had an undefeated team that year. The final meet was the Heptagonal Games, which was for athletes from all the colleges now known as the Ivy League, except that Brown was not yet a part of the group. The meet was to be held in Palmer Stadium, and both Bonthron and I were invited to be officials. I traveled down to Princeton in the morning in time to have lunch with the Bonthrons at their house on Alexander Street. The food and the talk were so good that time passed quickly, and suddenly one of us looked up at the clock and saw that we only had 10 minutes before we were due at our respective posts.

The Bonthron house was about half a mile from Palmer Stadium; covering that distance in a very few minutes presented no problem for Bonny, even though he was no longer a competitive runner. But I have never been known as Speedy Schwed. We set off at what was for him a dogtrot, but for me a major athletic effort. Bill chatted amiably all the way, but I, normally a garrulous chap, needed every bit of breath for this nonstop run. We did make it just on time, and I recovered sufficiently to carry out my tabulation chores at the javelin throw and to enjoy seeing Princeton win the Heptagonals. There were no official timers clocking my half-mile run, but I know very well that it would be listed as my "personal best" for the distance. Of course, I had an excellent pacesetter.

Later on I was thinking about what a grueling experience it had been for me. After all, I was a tennis player who covered the court pretty well. I wasn't a bad athlete at all, and I was still in my twenties, but how hard I had had to work to keep pace with a great runner who was only dogtrotting. I managed to do it, but it was no fun. The Bonthron clock had indicated that we had 10 minutes, but we wanted to get there before anybody had to start looking for us, so I'd estimate that we covered the half mile in around four minutes. That's a crawl for a track man but it was a super effort for me.

I only tried to do something comparable one other time, and that was even more humiliating. Admittedly, it happened in 1979, by which time I was no longer in my late twenties but late sixties. It was just before I was about to publish Bill Rodgers's book, *Marathoning*, and Rodgers, the country's star marathoner then, was trying to win his fourth consecutive New York City marathon. Of course, I ardently wanted him to do so: apart from the wonderful promotion it would give to the launching of the book, I had gotten to know Bill well and to admire him.

I made my way to my favorite spot to see the marathoners go by each year, which is just above the entrance to Central Park at Eighty-fifth Street and Fifth Avenue. It's a couple of miles from the finish line, but you're not jammed up among the huge crowds that press anywhere near the finish tape. With rare exceptions the person who is leading at that point will be the winner, and you actually are close enough to the runners to see them and be seen, with no restraining ropes holding you back. When Bill Rodgers showed up on the stretch of road north of where I was standing, running alone and obviously hundreds of yards ahead of the next runner, I jubilantly pranced out a yard onto the outer rim of the road, which many people do in the excitement of rooting for their favorites. It in no way interferes with the runners, all of whom at that stage are hugging the inside of the road in order to cut down the distance they still have to run. I waved gleefully to Bill and shouted his name and, by all that's holy, he recognized me, and grinned, and waved back. As he came alongside I tried to run opposite him for a short stretch. It was a mighty short stretch. A world-class marathoner runs over 26 miles at a five-minutes-per-mile pace, and that's what Bill was doing. I couldn't keep up with him for more than a block, and I knew I never could have.

So what else is new?

CHAPTER 17

Freddy and Le Sport

A better funny man than athlete

My elder brother, Fred, was quite a good golfer—something like a 6-handicap man—but although he dabbled at tennis now and then, it certainly was not his game. I remember with equal portions of amusement and affection two sports stories that relate to him, one in golf and one in tennis.

We made a golfing threesome one day, Fred and I and our mutual friend Jack. Jack had turned away to shield the cigarette he was lighting just as Fred drove a ball off the first tee. The ball zoomed high into the air but midway in flight hooked sharply to the left and sailed out of bounds. Jack, who hadn't seen any of this, of course, got his cigarette lit, turned, and said, "Sounded good."

Fred drew himself up and responded imperiously, "Thank you, but I am not auditioning for a concert recital!"

The tennis incident took place one summer in Connecticut when four of us went out to play a little casual doubles. Fred was by far the weakest player and I the strongest, so we teamed up against the other two. Shortly after we started, Fred and I were both at net when one of our opponents tossed a weak lob over Fred's head, which he made no effort to hit and which landed no deeper than midcourt. Loving brother that I was I nevertheless felt impelled to break the rule that a person should never criticize his doubles partner during a game. I did so with some clarity.

"For crying out loud, Freddy! How about getting the lead out? The idea is to win points! If you had taken two—possibly only one—step back while that ball was in the air, you'd have been in a perfect position to smash it away easily!"

Fred was almost 10 years older than I, and he was ever a patient and explicit teacher to his kid brother. He explained.

"You see, Pete, I am a most finely attuned physical specimen. The moment—the *very moment*—that lob was hit, my brain, backed by my keen competitive instinct, flashed a message that went *instantly* to my legs, feet, arms, hands, fingers, and every cell in my being. The message was 'Turn your left shoulder to the net as you take two half-skip glides back toward the baseline, follow the flight of the ball with the extended fingers of your left arm tracing its path in order to observe its descent with complete assurance and accuracy, prepare your racquet for the hit at the same time by getting your right elbow up head high and cocking your right wrist to drop the head of the racquet into the 'back-scratching' position, and at exactly the right moment leap into the air and, like unleashing a coiled spring, explode all your weight into the smash, meeting the ball high up and slightly in front of your body and snapping your wrist over the top of the stroke so as to powder the ball away at an angle that no opponent could possibly ever reach.'

"All of that transpired like lightning, Pete, and equally instantaneously there flashed back a message to my brain from my legs, feet, arms, hands, fingers, and every cell in my being. The message was 'Who? *Me?*' "

CHAPTER 18

Put Up or Shut Up

A very frustrating story

As a child of the Great Depression who saw his beloved high-stakes gambling father die broke, I never had the urge to do anything more, with respect to betting, than the most mild sort of speculation. When I have played cards it has been for small stakes, and when I have made an occasional bet on a sporting event, it has been with a friend, and payment of the bet has consisted of one of us picking up the tab at our next luncheon together. Pop, on the other hand, made a life of gambling heavily, both in his business and in certain recreational sidelines. A well-known Wall Street figure with a seat on the old Curb Exchange (now the American Exchange), Pop was not a traditional broker with an eye for interesting long-term investments in soundly managed companies. He was a speculator—known as a wire trader—who would buy or sell thousands of shares of a company in which he had no interest, in the belief that the price would go up or down a fraction of a point in the next few minutes. Whether he bought or sold depended upon what his betting instincts suggested to him was likely to happen—not upon market research. He got a lot of action that way every day and made—and lost—a great deal of money regularly in the process.

But my father's real pleasure was in betting away from Wall Street, and it has been written of him that during his flush periods, he always pinned two $1,000 bills into an inside pocket of his suit; he was afraid he might be offered an attractive bet and wouldn't have the cash on hand to cover it. Pop's specialty was betting on matters of opinion: what horse would win a race; what team, a sporting event; what candidate, a gubernatorial or presidential election. He actually was so well-known for making book on important elections that the odds he quoted were printed in the papers as the official odds, quite the way the Las Vegas line is quoted today on professional football games. The only area in which he bet heavily on his own skills was in extremely high-stakes auction bridge games—this was in the days before contract bridge. Since he was a player of very great skill, he may well have done better at that than at any other form of wagering.

All of this about my father is a preamble to introducing a man who may have rivaled Pop for the number of gambling genes packed into his system. His name was Jack Goodman, and I was lucky enough to be his very close friend for more than 25 years until he died, prematurely, at the age of 48. Jack, in addition to being the most charming and funny and the wisest of companions, was marvelously adept at just about everything he tackled, and it was a constant joy to be with him. Certainly we competed against each other in some things. I could beat him at tennis about as badly as he could beat me at golf, but since those were foregone conclusions, we never bet on them. Also, Jack was the vice-president, editor-in-chief, and advertising director of Simon & Schuster when that firm hired me after World War II, and he had much more money to bet, and a much greater inclination to do so, than I ever did. The amounts he bet were not in the same league with some of my father's wagers, but they were much too rich for my blood and for my salary at the time.

Jack's gambling passions tended more in the direction of backing his own skills, rather than his opinions. An even better contract bridge player than my father had been an auction bridge player, Jack plunged into the same sort of fabulously high-stakes games and did very well. He was a player with a national reputation and was a onetime co-winner with his partner of the Vanderbilt Cup. Jack bet heavily not only on his bridge game, but also on poker and backgammon, two other games at which he excelled; he was more than eager to risk a sizable bet on himself in just about any other pursuit that happened along, as will become evident in the anecdote that follows.

Right through the 1930's and 1940's contract bridge flourished to an extent that makes today's continued and widespread preoccupation with the game look mild indeed. Contract bridge is still big stuff throughout this nation, but there are certainly lots of people who have never played it at all. Half a century or so ago, playing at least an acceptable game of bridge was more of a social requirement than knowing how to dance decently, and playing a top-notch game of bridge was an "open sesame" to very exalted circles. Jack Goodman was a brilliant player, as were three other people at Simon & Schuster, including Richard Simon, one of the two bosses. So it was natural in this era of national bridge frenzy that the house should seek out the man who had succeeded Ely Culbertson as the greatest and most successful authority on the game, P. Hal Sims. They persuaded Sims to write a book about his system, *Money Contract*, which introduced a new bidding system that replaced Culbertson's and became a huge best-seller.

Hal Sims, a tall, elephantine figure of a man who must have weighed close to 300 pounds, became a good friend of Jack's in the course of publishing the book. Sims and his wife, Dorothy, had a palatial summer house on the shore at Deal, New Jersey, and each weekend it became a camping ground for the many people Hal invited there, almost all of whom qualified for invitations because they were high-stakes bridge players. Jack had a standing invitation, and one weekend, just before we were going to take a golfing vacation together for a couple of weeks, Jack thought it would be fun for the two of us to go to Deal first, and take off from there. I was hesitant. Would I be welcome? Jack replied that the house was so immense and so informal that Hal and Dorothy never recognized half the people who were there, and I was not to worry about it. There were no set meals: an immense, hotel-style refrigerator was always piled full of wonderful things to eat, and people simply grabbed what they wanted and went off to eat it, some in dinner jackets and others in sweat suits or bathing trunks, depending upon their plans.

"Hal will be glad you came along," Jack said. "He's seen you around at Simon & Schuster and knows you're my friend. You're a good backgammon player, and while I'm playing bridge you can certainly pick up a game at stakes you can afford. There are always hangers-on around, who are not that different from you and come to enjoy the atmosphere rather than to gamble. And I'll make sure that Dorothy digs up a bed for you, or at least a cot in my room, and if it has to be the last, I'll play you a game of backgammon to see who gets the bed."

So I went, and Jack turned out to be right. That first night while Jack played in a Sims-dominated bridge game, I fiddled the evening away pleasantly enough at backgammon with a mild fellow and at the end of it found myself some ten dollars richer. Gratified, I wandered into the bridge room in time to see the scores being totaled and now saw, to my distress, that Jack had taken just about the most catastrophic shellacking I had ever seen him suffer. At the stakes I knew these men played for, he must have lost at least a half a year of my rent in one night. I knew that Jack was in Hal's class as a bridge player, so he must have had an abominable run of luck, but Jack was always a sportsman and had nothing to say as we retired to our rooms for the night except to tell me that he had arranged a tennis game for us the following morning.

"We'll be partners," Jack told me, "and I've got a bet that we can beat Hal and some guy from the tennis club, who will partner him. You're really a good player, Pete, and I'm not bad, and I can't think anyone can carry Hal as a partner if we keep hitting every ball to him. He's so big and fat that he can scarcely waddle—he won't be able to cover half of the court at all."

Well, it turned out that he didn't have to. Except when he himself was serving or being the receiver, when of necessity he had to hit one ball from the baseline area, Hal simply took up a position at net without budging whenever his partner was serving or receiving. He made no attempt to poach to the side or go back for a lob, but just let his energetic partner run for and retrieve any ball he couldn't reach easily. Being well over six feet tall, however, he could reach a lot of balls, and when he could reach them he absolutely murdered them. Whenever he became the server or receiver, he made that one rear-court stroke, and then walked, did not run (just as you're instructed to do in case of fire in a theater) to that same rigid post at net, leaving it to his partner to handle things long enough to allow him to get there. If a return was hit directly at him as he strolled up, he was able to volley it back well enough. Anyhow, when the one set we'd agreed to play was over, he and his partner had nosed out Jack and me. Hal complained throughout that he was too old, and that his eyesight was now so poor that he could scarcely see the ball, which is why the match was limited to one set. But if he didn't see the ball any other time, he certainly seemed to see it very well whenever it came close to him!

I saw Jack pull out his checkbook, write briefly in it, and hand over a small, rectangular piece of paper to Sims. I figured that this must have been a comparatively minor loss, but I still regretted that my own efforts to win a little something back for Jack hadn't been good enough.

Jack perked up considerably when Sims suggested 18 holes of golf for the afternoon. Although he knew that Hal was a very good golfer, likely to shoot in the mid-70's, Jack was just about as good as that himself, and his partner was to be a friend who played golf regularly and surely couldn't be anywhere near as abominable a player as I, who almost never played. Hal looked at me and said that a fellow who played as nice a tennis game as I did couldn't be as bad a golfer as I claimed to be. I told him he was wrong. He said he'd take me on as a partner anyway.

It was a very close match all around the course. A point was scored for best ball, and a point for aggregate, each hole. Jack and his partner won aggregate most of the time, because my score was often too bad to be offset by Hal's invariably good one, but Hal won the lion's share of best ball despite Jack's good play. We came to the last hole all even, and with all of us having putted out before Hal, the situation was that he could win the entire match if he could hole the 10-foot putt that faced him, for that would be best ball and would tie aggregate. But if he missed the putt, he'd lose the match, because in that case low ball would only be a tie, while aggregate would be lost. Not an easy putt to make under such circumstances, and Hal explained why it was particularly hard all the time he was lining it up, and then in the many seconds while he took his stance and leaned over the ball. He said it was tragic how badly his sight had gone off; he no longer could make out the undulations of the green, and even the outline of the cup was fuzzy. Talking all the while, he then drew back his putter and stroked the ball unerringly into the dead center of the cup. Jack pulled out his checkbook over drinks in the clubhouse this time.

The next morning Hal suggested that we all take a little stroll on the boardwalk at Asbury Park, since the heavy action at the bridge table wouldn't be starting until late in the day. This time there were only the three of us, and I was enjoying the cool ocean breezes, even if Jack was probably burning up at his three successive losses. But suddenly he seemed to brighten up. We were passing a billiard parlor and pool room. Jack, I knew, was a good enough amateur billiards player to have competed, and not done too badly, in college competition.

"How about a little straight rail billiards, Hal?" he inquired.

"Oh, Jack, I'm too old," said Sims. "My hands shake, my sight is all but gone, and I've no touch at all. Once I could play this game fairly well, but I haven't done anything with it for years and years. I couldn't keep up with you."

"Come on, Hal," urged Jack. "It'll be fun, and you've got to give me a chance to get some of my money back."

"Well, all right, but it'll be a form of charity from me to you. How much do you want to play for?" asked Sims.

A stake was arranged, we all repaired to the billiard table, and Jack and Hal flipped a coin to see who would start a match for 100 points. Jack won the toss, which at least broke his string of successive losses and perhaps foretold better things to come. He stepped up to the table and ran off 17 caroms before he missed, which is an extremely good run for an amateur billiards player. Well satisfied, he stepped back and surrendered the table to Sims, who, muttering all the way about his inability to see things clearly enough, proceeded to knock off a run of 22. Good competitor though he was, Jack obviously was badly shaken. He ran off four on his next turn but left the balls in an almost impossible position after that and missed on his attempt for a fifth. Sims took over and ran 26, and to all intents and purposes the match was over. At one stage Jack himself made a run of slightly more than 20, but Sims closed out his 100 points before Jack ever reached 60. No money or checks passed hands just then, but I knew the accounting could not be far off. We walked out again onto the boardwalk, and suddenly there was the sound of rifle shots. I stole a sidewise look at Jack—I could guess what was coming. Jack had actually been the New York Metropolitan collegiate rifle champion a few years before. My guess was right.

"Come on Hal, let's do some target shooting. What do you say?"

Sims paused and pondered. Then he responded. "These places are so shoddy and dirty, Jack, and their rifles aren't that good. You wouldn't want to shoot here. But I have a range and some good rifles set up back of the house at Deal. Let's go there and shoot."

Jack may have been a gallant and an impetuous man, but stupid he certainly was not. He grinned wryly.

"Hal," he said, "if you have your own rifles and a range back at your place, never mind. I'll wait for the bridge game tonight."

CHAPTER 19

The Incredible Brownie

No one else ever did what Mary K. Browne did

"One of the most astonishing events in the history of sports took place last week, when Mary Kimball Browne of Los Angeles defeated Nancy Lopez in the semifinal round of the Womens National Golf Championship, after meeting and triumphing over two other great stars, Pat Bradley and Amy Alcott, earlier in the week. What makes her feat so remarkable is that only two weeks ago Browne battled the greatest woman tennis player in the world, Martina Navratilova, to a virtual standoff in the semifinals of the Women's National Tennis Tournament and, in finally losing to her 6–4, 4–6, 6–3, gave Navratilova by far her toughest match of the year."

If you read that paragraph in your newspaper's sports section today, could you possibly believe it? Both golf and tennis at a championship level played by the same person, one within two weeks of the other! Mary Kimball Browne? Who's she?

Yet the fact is that Miss Browne once did parallel these incredible dual accomplishments or, to return to actual facts, she did the exact equivalent in her own era. Simply substitute the 1924 women champions in golf and tennis, Glenna Collett and Helen Wills, for Nancy and Martina. They were the two women athletes whose fame was comparable to the male immortals of the time, Bobby Jones, Bill Tilden, Babe Ruth, Jack Dempsey, Paavo Nurmi, Red

127

Grange, Glenna Collett and Helen Wills were each virtually invincible at her respective game, but the now forgotten Mary K. Browne in that year achieved something that has never been matched before or since. She had been a world-class tennis player for years, so her showing against Helen Wills wasn't too surprising. But she was almost a fledgling golfer who had never played in a major golf tournament before, and her defeat of Glenna Collett—the only match Glenna lost all year and one of the very few she ever lost—ranks as one of the greatest upsets that sport has ever witnessed.

I thought her feat so unique that it deserved retelling today, when so few would remember it. In checking the background, I came across an official statistic that seemed to reveal an almost equally startling fact about our heroine. If it were shown to be true, it would completely change the hitherto accepted status of another modern tennis champion.

Way back in 1912, a dozen years before her dual exploits on the tennis courts and the golf course, Mary K. Browne won the National Women's tennis singles title, and the doubles and the mixed doubles as well. But this impressive hat trick is only incidental to the surprising discovery I unearthed in the records, which sent me off in search of more about this legendary lady. *Every* record book—from the official United States Tennis Association yearbooks to the several encyclopedias of tennis—listed Browne's birth date as 1897. That would have made her 15 years old in 1912, and if that were the case, then Tracy Austin was not the youngest champion in tennis history. Tracy, like the youngest champion before her, Maureen Connolly, was 16 when she won the U.S. Open Women's Singles championship in 1979.

With all due affection for Tracy, it would have made quite a story in itself to establish Browne as the rightful claimant to the title of youngest champion, but from the beginning I had an idea that something was wrong. I couldn't believe that in 1951, when Maureen Connolly was hailed as the youngest champion ever, someone—even Mary Browne herself, who was alive then—

wouldn't have contested the fact. I tried checking the matter with obvious sources and got nowhere. So I thought I'd try to see if I might have better luck on Miss Browne's old home turf in the far West. A telephone call to the Southern California Tennis Association was answered by a most helpful woman, Doris Cook, who suggested that I call a lady named Rosalie Vance, a neighbor and close friend of Mary Browne's, who had been with her when she died.

Marvelous Miss Vance first put me onto a man named Kenneth Kenneth-Smith (*sic*). The less important thing about him from my standpoint was that he had once been married to Mary K. Browne. The vital piece of information he gave me was that he and Mary were classmates and tennis partners at Los Angeles Polytechnic High School in the early years of the century and that she definitely was born in 1891— *not* 1897. I hope that this article will act as a piece of revisionist history and that the record books in the future will be changed, because Mary K. Browne was not 15 when she won those 1912 championships—she was 21. Tracy Austin is indeed the youngest champion ever, and she is entitled not to be bothered by some probing witling, like me, questioning the facts in the years to come.

Youngest or not, Mary was a real and extraordinary tennis champion. In that first year she swept the field at the Philadelphia Cricket Club courts, winning the finals of all three events in which women played, and all on the same day, June 15, 1912. She defeated a fine player, Eleanor Sears, in the singles, 6–4, 6–2, and teamed with Dorothy Green to win the women's doubles in three sets. Her partner in the mixed doubles was R. Norris (Dick) Williams, a great star then and later, who only two months before this tournament had been on board the doomed *Titanic* and had been fished out of the waters of the icy North Atlantic.

In 1913 and in 1914 Browne repeated this feat, again winning all three titles, but she had a new mixed doubles partner. He was a young college player who showed promise but who didn't become really good for another half a dozen years; the newspaper accounts imply that Mary more or less "carried" him to victory. His name was Bill Tilden.

After 1914 Mary Browne dropped out of big-time tennis for a long period. She reappeared at Forest Hills in the 1921 tournament and went right through the draw to the finals of the singles, where after winning the first set from the reigning champion, Molla Mallory, she eventually lost. But in the women's doubles event she and her old partner from 1913 and 1914, Louise Williams , once again took the championship title.

Once again Mary disappeared from national competition, until 1924. By this time Helen Wills had started her domination that was to last for more than a decade. No one gave her even the semblance of a battle throughout the tournament except for Mary K. Browne in the semifinals, in which, as mentioned earlier, Wills squeezed out a 6–4, 4–6, 6–3 victory that left both women so exhausted that it was minutes before either had the strength to come to the net for the traditional handshake. An indication of how good Helen Wills had become by then is apparent from what she did to Molla Mallory the next day in the final. Wills swept past Mallory easily, winning 6–1, 6–3, and as a result Browne was ranked number two to Wills in the nation, Mallory having to be content with number three. For Brownie's fans, her marvelous performance, at the age of 33, against the invincible young Wills was inspiring but not altogether surprising. After all, Browne had long been a top-notch tennis player; she was famous for being just about the first woman to forsake the then customary baseline game and attack and volley at net as often as possible.

Two weeks later Mary really did amaze the sports world. She had taken up golf in the years since 1914, but only in a desultory way. She really didn't have the credentials to enter the women's golf championship, but somehow she qualified for the draw and won the preliminary match-play rounds that took her into the semifinals. There, she tied the great Glenna on the 18th hole and beat her on the first extra hole with what the *New York Times* termed "the two most spectacular and miraculous shots ever to decide a championship."

Mary K. Browne never figured in championship golf again, and she probably didn't try. Her real game was tennis, and in the following year, 1925, she once again won the National Women's Doubles title, this time with Helen Wills as partner. In 1926 the first professional tennis tour was organized by C. C. (Cash and Carry) Pyle, which featured four great stars, two men and two women. The men were Vincent Richards, a superstar of that era, and Howard Kinsey. The women were Suzanne Lenglen, the incomparable French player, who was the only female in the world rated higher than Helen Wills, and—guess who? Mary K. Browne.

After that time (if you're still counting years), Mary was in her late thirties and once again dropped out of the public view. What happened to her then? I got the answer from Alice Marble, who was the best woman player in the world in the years leading up to 1940 and who might well have been rated the best of all time had her career not been cut short prematurely by illness. Alice, a very close friend of Brownie's, revealed that Mary turned teaching professional, for both tennis and golf. Later she became a very successful and much sought-after portrait painter, but she always continued to play the games at which she so excelled. Alice Marble became a pretty good golfer herself, and she was with Mary Browne when she shot a 75 on an admittedly not-too-demanding golf course, but Mary was then 75 years old!

In 1957 Mary Kimball Browne was elected to the Tennis Hall of Fame and came to New York City en route to the ceremony at Newport, Rhode Island. Kenneth Kenneth-Smith, who had not seen her since their high school days together half a century before except to watch her play, telephoned her and asked her if he could drive her up to Newport. Mary said she'd enjoy that, so they took off and renewed their friendship on the ride. She was 66 years old then, and he about a year older. They stood together during the ceremony that marked Mary's induction into the Hall of Fame and then, very shortly afterward, stood up together again for another ceremony—their wedding ceremony. After five years they separated amicably, and remained solid friends until Brownie's death in 1971.

Mary K. Browne is a name that should live on in sports lore, but for Tracy Austin's benefit, let the historians get her birth date right from now on. If they do, you owe me one, Tracy!

CHAPTER 20

Every Dog Has Its Day

The year when chess took over the sports page

There are perhaps 10 sports that throughout this century have consistently attracted intense spectator interest and coverage by the media in the U.S. Alphabetically, they are baseball, bowling, boxing, football, golf, hockey, horse racing, skiing, tennis, and track. Other sports appeal to a bemused and enthusiastic, but small group of fans yet once every four years excite national interest when they become centerpieces of television's coverage of the Olympics. Such sports are gymnastics, rowing, swimming, water polo, weight lifting, wrestling, volleyball, and yachting.

There is one notable omission from these two lists—soccer. That is because the popularity of soccer on the one hand, and its lack of popularity on the other, is one of the outstanding paradoxes of American sport.

Without question, soccer, or football as it is known outside the United States, is far and away the most popular international sport. In Europe and in South America it's not at all uncommon for games to draw crowds of 150,000. A considerably more pleasant game to play than American football, soccer is a very big participant sport in our schools and colleges. But as far as filling the grandstands goes, soccer has been a failure in this country at both the college and the professional levels. An all-out attempt to change this a few years ago included importing great foreign stars, such as Pele, to play on American teams. For one season a few games actually did fill the stadiums. But it was, like Camelot, only one brief shining moment. Today the American interest in professional soccer, and the crowds who attend games, are right back to the low level they were prior to the Pele days.

There are several reasons for this, none of them very good but all of them understandable. A primary factor is the necessity to compete for attention with such a popular sport as American football. Then, this country has never developed strong enough national teams to launch a credible attack on the World Cup, which is to soccer what the Olympic Games are to other sports, and Americans are slow to evince any interest in sports in which Americans don't excel. It doesn't matter if a sport is wildly popular everywhere else in the world: some American has to pop up as a world beater before our imagination and enthusiasm are aroused. That is what happened in gymnastics. Until we started producing a few champions of our own, like Kurt Thomas, Cathy Rigby, and Mary Lou Retton, Americans hardly knew that the sport of gymnastics existed. If they thought about it at all, it was likely to be with resentment every four years at the time of the Olympics, when the Russians would win as many gold medals in gymnastics as the Americans did in what they considered the "real events"— track and field and swimming. Today gymnastics has become a wildly popular spectator sport, and Mary Lou Retton has become as much of an idol as Martina Navratilova. The same is true of volleyball, which was never regarded here as much of a sport except to have fun on the beach, until American teams started winning in world competition.

But no American team, nor even an American individual, has ever shone internationally at soccer. Also the game is continuous, without the many timeouts that infest American football, and there's no opportunity for advertising sponsors to get in their messages frequently during a television broadcast. So no national television network is interested in soccer. (I wrote that the reasons for soccer's failure to achieve the popularity it deserves were not good, but were understandable.)

In addition to the perennial favorites and the occasional favorites, are those sports that win their share of recognition for a time, then recede. Some come back again after a while, but some disappear, seemingly forever. Among this last group, six-day bicycle racing is a prime example. Believe it or not, there was a day in the early part of the century when that sport's public used to jam the old Madison Square Garden to capacity during an event's final stages, and filled a substantial portion of the arena prior to that each day and night, continuously, for six days. People used to drop in at any time of day and spend a few hours. Salesmen might come in the morning before making their first calls. Workers in the neighborhood would bring in paper-bag lunches and munch them over the noon hours while watching the cyclists go round and round. A particularly popular time was late at night, after a party or the theater, when, almost like on New Year's Eve, late revelers would stick around until daybreak and hunger pangs reminded them it was time for breakfast. Now that an American, Greg Lemond, has won the Tour de France, the world's most prestigious bicycle race, I suppose it's conceivable that Americans may become more prominent in the sport, and some promoter may try to bring back the indoor six-day bicycle race. I wouldn't bet on it, though.

It took a legitimate American sports idol like Tommy Hitchcock to make international polo matches into major sports news and attractions in the U.S. back in the twenties and thirties. Now polo is like my own pet sport, badminton. There are still those who love it and, in the case of polo, can afford to play it, but far from making headlines in the sports section, it's lucky if it's reported at all, and the opportunity to see a polo match is rare indeed for most Americans. Polo has become almost as much purely a participant sport as croquet, which has had quite a remarkable renaissance in popularity recently. It's one of those sports that come and go and come back again, like ladies' fashions.

I have tender memories of billiards, the topic that forms the background for a forthcoming chapter about the incomparable Willie Hoppe. But I'm afraid that true billiards—played on a table without pockets—has virtually disappeared forever in its several forms. Pool—played on a table with pockets—has replaced it almost completely, more's the pity. Pool is a fine game, but billiards was fine art!

What other sport enjoyed a crest of unaccustomed popularity and public interest and then faded into obscurity again? Let me think, once again alphabetically. Archery? No. Bobsledding? No. Canoeing? No. Ah, I have it, if you'll concede it's a sport. Chess!

Since that concession seems to be up to me, I will concede it, because what happened in 1972 in the world of chess is truly something to remember and marvel at again: the historic match between Bobby Fisher of the United States and Boris Spassky of Russia, in Reykjavik, Iceland, for the world chess championship. That match, with its 21 fiercely contested games before Fischer finally won, took a couple of months and was televised all over the world. It was incredible how we all sat up for hour after hour to watch the coverage, when none of us were chess players of any skill, and some of us barely knew more than the moves. That match obviously was fascinating to the world's few million true chess players and enthusiasts, but it also became an unbelievable sensation for hundreds of millions of neophytes, and even non-players. For pure mass appeal it can claim to be termed the greatest sports event of the decade, and perhaps of all time. Certainly, over the course of the match, more people turned on their television sets to watch it than saw the Frazier-Ali fight in Manila.

The Fisher-Spassky chess encounter, even more than the United States soccer season when Pele's presence drew huge crowds, strikes me as the prime example of a sport, or game, suddenly scaling a peak of unaccustomed interest and popularity, only to recede subsequently to a normal level. When the next world chess championship was held in 1986, between Gary Kasparov and Anatoly Karpov, it received some coverage both in the papers and on PBS television, but any passionate interest in it in this country was confined to chess zealots. The chess boom had been tremendous, but it had come and gone.

I was lucky enough to have the 1972 sensation benefit me. I happened to be in London the summer just before the match, on my annual scouting trip looking for foreign books that would be good for Simon & Schuster's list. A man from *The Chess Player*, an English magazine, called me up one day. He said he had heard I was in town, knew S&S's reputation, and wanted to see me to discuss an exciting publishing project having to do with the impending Fisher-Spassky match. Of course, I was well aware that this would be a big thing, even though I never could have imagined how big, so I was interested.

He came to my hotel and told me that *The Chess Player* had engaged a Yugoslavian grand master named Svetozar Gligoric to cover the matches in Iceland and transmit the results, along with his commentary, within hours of each game. Gligoric was completely fluent in English and was an experienced chess writer and analyst. *The Chess Player* intended to set type and make printing plates throughout the weeks that the long match would be going on, and at the end of the final session and upon receipt of Gligoric's final report, complete the makeready form for actually printing pages and go to press immediately. They expected to have finished and bound books in bookstores in Great Britain within 48 hours of the conclusion of the match. Was I interested in doing something with it as far as United States publication was concerned?

I certainly was, even though at the time I never dreamed how completely absorbing the match would be to Americans, or how hugely successful such a book would be. But I was aware that if we were to have any success, time was of the essence. Such a book simply had to be published right on the heels of the match. So I made a deal that *The Chess Player* would print an extra 25,000 copies with the Simon & Schuster imprint on the first run and would air-freight them direct from the bindery so that we'd receive them at very nearly the same moment as the British publisher. For a chess book, 25,000 seemed like a lot of copies, but just in case of a miracle, I also obtained the right to offset the British edition, which means to photograph it and make our own plates from which we could produce more copies.

The 25,000 copies were gone within a day or two after they were shipped into the stores in the U.S.A. After Fisher's victory and the immense excitement it generated, that was only too predictable, so we made plates and were ready to go to press the moment it was evident that more copies would be needed. We weren't out of stock more than a couple of days, and a lot more copies were needed throughout the next few weeks as excitement over Fisher's victory continued unabated. Approximately half a million more copies, to be fairly exact!

The entire affair demonstrates dramatically how chauvinistic, in a patriotic sense, Americans are about sports. As long as an American, Bobby Fisher, was challenging for world domination, and succeeding, chess became of major interest to the entire nation. Once that was over, chess went back to what it had been before—the best of board games to play, but certainly not a major spectator sport.

Meanwhile, what ever happened to Bobby Fisher? He retired to a California religious cult, became a recluse who never sees even his closest old friends, and only plays chess, when he does, with a computer!

CHAPTER 21

Some Like It Hot— and Some Do Not!

*Twenty-five laps around the track
in the broiling 100° sun*

When a person reaches a ripe old age and goes into "overtime" with respect to his sports memories, the ones that come first to mind are the sensational, the dramatic, the record-breaking. If someone had ever asked me, "Quick! Without thinking about it too much, what was the most memorable sports event that took place in your lifetime?" I would probably have rattled off a dozen thrilling games or an individual performance that would draw a nod of recognition and possible agreement. I might have named Bobby Thomson's "home run heard around the world," which won the National League pennant for the New York Giants over the Brooklyn Dodgers in 1951, or Roger Bannister's breakthrough four-minute mile. Perhaps I'd have nominated the seventh and decisive game of the 1970 basketball championships, when the New York Knicks beat the Los Angeles Lakers to win the series four games to three. Remember? Willis Reed, their captain and center, had a severe leg injury and wasn't supposed to play at all, but he ran onto the court at the beginning of the game and played brilliantly for a few minutes while the Knick fans, including me, screamed their lungs out. That was enough to inspire the rest of

that superb team, including Walt Frazier, Dave DeBusschere, Bill
Bradley, and Dick Barnett, to join Reed in pulling off the "miracle
on Thiry-third Street," which was the title of the book that was
written about the event.

I would have been hard put not to nominate stunning upsets like
the victory of the United States Olympic hockey team over the
Russians in 1980, or Joe Namath's New York Jets' beating the
Baltimore Colts in the third Super Bowl in 1968. Bobby Jones's
Grand Slam of golf in 1930, and Jack Nicklaus's twentieth major
championship win at the Masters tournament in 1986 might have
occurred to me, along with several other equally dazzling events
that stand out in sports history. Upon reflection, however, I find
that any of these answers would be wrong. The key word in the
original question is *memorable*. Not the most exciting, or the most
historic, or the most headline-deserving, but the most *memorable*—unique and absolutely unforgettable.

With that thought in mind, I would have to say unqualifiedly that
the most memorable event took place in 1959 at Franklin Field,
Philadelphia, during the first dual track meet between the United
States and Russia ever held in this country. No one who wasn't
there will have any memory of the event, the 10,000-meter run,
for it was one of the least competitive and by most standards one of
the dullest ones ever held—but no one who was actually present in
Philadelphia that day is likely ever to forget it.

If you were present you will recall that after you fought your way
through the crowd to find the precious seat that you had reserved
by mail application long in advance for this sellout meet, you
probably couldn't sit down on it. The official temperature in the
shade that day was up in the nineties, but in the grandstand, where
a blazing sun beat down from a cloudless sky in mid-July, it was
well over 100°. Without some insulating material to separate your
posterior from the fiery-hot seat, your goose quite literally would
have been cooked.

I had a break in that respect. I had a good friend who was a sportswriter on a major newspaper, and he had two passes for seats in the press box. Knowing my passion for track and field, he invited me to join him, and while it was mighty hot there, too, at least we had protection from the relentless sun.

If it was hot in the stands and in the press box, it was more so out on the field. Such conditions were clearly going to be hard on the distance runners, especially for the competitors in the 10,000 meters, the longest event scheduled for this meet. The runners would have to travel almost 25 circuits of the quarter-mile track to complete the 6.2 mile distance. Although the Americans were favored to win the men's team competition, they were not expected to do well in the 10,000 meters. Traditionally they had dominated the shorter races, and the Russians had taken the longer ones. It had been thus the previous year in Russia, in the first and only other dual meet between the rival national track powers of the time; aficionados who knew the situation were reasonably sure that history was about to repeat itself.

For this meet each country was to have just two representatives in each event, and in the 10,000 meters the two Russians virtually had been conceded first and second place even before running the race. Aleksey Desyatchikov was recognized as a world-class runner at the distance, and his Estonian teammate, Hubert Pyarnakivi, was rated close behind him. American boosters had a faint hope that Max Truex, the tenacious little 5'5" runner, might nip Pyarnakivi for second place on sheer guts, but no one would have cared to make such a prediction. The other American, Bob Soth, a 26-year-old schoolteacher, was practically unknown to the crowd. He had qualified to run in this event by finishing as the number two American in the Amateur Athletic Union championships, but most of the other better-known American distance runners had not competed in the 10,000 meters at the AAU meet, choosing instead to run in the 5,000 meters or the steeplechase.

The "official" results of the 10,000-meter run on that hot day in Philadelphia are ludicrously misleading.

1. Desyatchikov, Soviet Union, 31:40.6
2. Pyarnakivi, Soviet Union, 33:13.4
3. Truex, United States, approximately 34:40.0
4. Soth, United States, did not finish. No score

Considering that the current world record for the 10,000 meters is only a little more than 27 minutes, and that even at that time, in 1959, Vladimir Kuts of Russia had run the distance in 28:30, there is nothing in these bare numbers to elicit more than a yawn from a track fan. Clearly, the times were incomprehensibly slow for runners of this calibre, with the second place man not within shouting distance of the winner, and the third finisher almost as far again behind him. That Soth didn't finish also seems surprising. You would think that in such a slow race, an inspired turtle might have been able to make some sort of showing; by not finishing at all, Soth cost the United States team the one point awarded for fourth place in an event.

But the numbers don't begin to tell the story of what took place on the track that broiling day. Far from finding it a dull race, I suspect that anyone who saw that half-hour drama will remember it long after memories of hair-raising finishes and world-record races have faded.

At the sound of the starter's gun, the two Russian runners took the lead, as expected. Truex didn't seem to want to stay with the pace, but Soth clung to the leaders heels and then, after eight laps, or two miles, moved out in front and took the lead. Soth continued to run the race of his life right through the three-mile mark, where he was timed at 14:24.3—an absolutely brilliant performance for him and a very good one for anybody at that time. Both Russians were close behind; the highly regarded Max Truex had fallen far back.

On the next lap both Desyatchikov and Pyarnakivi passed Soth, who continued to hang on gamely but was visibly beginning to struggle. Max Truex apparently had given up trying to be competitive and was only going through the motions to finish, and so score a fourth-place point for the U.S. team.

Desyatchikov was the leader after four miles, having covered the distance faster than ever previously recorded in this country. He had a good 30-yard lead over Pyarnakivi, who was approximately the same distance ahead of Soth. Then Soth seemed to get a second wind: he stretched out and moved past Pyarnakivi into second place. Once Pyarnakivi had been passed he started to labor badly and to fall back rapidly. Both leaders lapped Truex soon afterward.

When Desyatchikov passed the five-mile mark, again setting a new American record for the distance, the outcome of the race seemed inevitable. Desyatchikov, who seemed capable of continuing to run all day at the 73 to 74 seconds per lap he had maintained so far, was going to win by a country mile. Soth, half a lap behind him, posed no threat, nor did it seem that Pyarnakivi could present any challenge to Soth, for he now was an equal distance back of him. You forget about Max Truex, who would probably be lapped a second time by Desyatchikov before this dreary race would be over.

And then it started to happen. Right after Soth passed five miles, with just a little over a mile to go, everyone in the stands was dumbfounded to see an astonishing change come over him. While continuing with all his heart to try to run, Soth straightened up completely from the forward tilt a runner's trunk maintains when in stride, and he even appeared to be leaning backward. His thighs and knees, moving up in slow motion to an extraordinary high level, enabled him to do no more than barely totter forward. Everything about his desperate attempts to keep running was weirdly unnatural, and the entire spectacle had the quality of a nightmare. Soth seemed to be running, if you could call it that, as if he were immersed in a tank filled with a very thick, viscous liquid.

Although no one appeared aware of it at the time, these reactions signal an impending physical collapse. The many officials on the field seemed as ignorant of what was happening as the most uninformed spectator. The steady, fast Desyatchikov was forgotten as all eyes in the stadium were fixed upon Soth, staggering, weaving a drunken path back and forth across the width of the track in super slow motion, trying through sheer determination and courage to continue running the race. He should have been stopped, of course, if anyone had had the knowledge and guts to do it. At the very least he should have been given water or doused with it, as is now always done along the route in marathon runs. But Soth was allowed to "run" over three laps in this condition, registering snail-like times of more than two minutes a lap, with no one making a move to stop the agony until he actually collapsed on the track, his head just missing the concrete edging of the rail. Finally—finally—people rushed to his aid and he was carried off the track to be treated.

No sooner had everyone's attention turned back to the race proper, where Desyatchikov was steaming along like an unflappable engine, than a new drama greeted their eyes. Pyarnakivi was starting to go into the same slow-motion, high-stepping, backward lean as Soth, and was barely moving. Incredibly, the same thing was happening to Truex, although with less visible agony. Neither man had yet been forced all the way into the grotesque movements that had overtaken Soth, but at just about the six-mile point, with less than one lap to go, Pyarnakivi's condition became so pathetic that he could hardly inch forward. He still had 300 yards to complete the distance, and he struggled on as best he could, but it looked as though he wouldn't be able to make it.

Meanwhile, the ineptitude of track officials was reaching new heights. They were so wrapped up in all the unprecedented goings-on that they had become confused about the lap count. Instead of sounding the gun at the proper time to signal one more lap to go, they let it go off as Desyatchikov actually *finished* his 10,000 meters. Desyatchikov, who knew track procedure and perhaps thought that numerical counting was different in English than

Russian, stolidly took an unnecessary extra circuit of the track. This resulted in his "official" but absurdly poor time of 31:40.6. He actually covered the prescribed distance in 30:29.9, a very respectable time in 1959—although even the slow "official" time was much more than sufficient to win this grotesque race handily.

Pyarnakivi continued to grope his way in a sort of blind stagger toward the finish line, making it just before collapsing completely into unconsciousness. The 376 yards that stretched before him after he passed the six-mile mark took him 1:54.8 to cover, but to his great credit, cover it he did. His time for the 10,000 meters was 33:13.4, and he was the only runner of all four contestants who ran the proper distance. We know that Soth dropped out, and Desyatchikov ran an extra quarter of a mile because of the incorrect sounding of the gun. But what happened to Max Truex?

Recognizing fairly early on that he had no chance of beating anyone that day, he had been taking it easy, and as a result he could fight off extreme physical distress. Desyatchikov obviously had run away with the race, but Truex had seen Soth collapse, and now he was seeing the same thing happen to Pyarnakivi when he still had most of his final lap to go: the Russian could scarcely move. Max was so far behind that catching up seemed hopeless, but he threw off his weariness and started to sprint unbelievably fast for a man who had run six miles on such a hot day, and he made up the better part of an entire lap to pass the virtually stationary Pyarnakivi well before the finish line. When he crossed that line he was timed at 32:49.6, or some 24 seconds faster than Pyarnakivi's time. So did Max Truex upset the form chart and win an unexpected and valuable second place for the United States in the 10,000-meter run? Yes, he did, but no, he did not.

As Truex crossed the proper finish line, Horace Ashenfelter, the 1952 Olympic steeplechase champion, who was acting as a judge on the curves, called out some advice to Truex. He shouted that the officials had become confused about the lap count, that Desyatchikov apparently had run an unnecessary extra lap, and that "just to be safe," Truex ought to do the same thing. So Max did jog one more circuit of the track, taking it good and easy, since the now collapsed Pyarnakivi was certainly out of contention, and no one else was left. But, of course, Truex took a lot longer completing that lap than the 24 seconds he already had on the Russian at the proper conclusion of the race. He was officially timed as finishing approximately in 34:40.0, considerably slower than Pyarnakivi's 33:13.4.

Even with all the drama and confusion, certain experienced track scribes alongside me in the press box were registering everything. Desyatchikov, the easy winner, had been timed at 29:19.9 as he passed the six-mile mark for an American record, and if his time for 10,000 meters was *really* 31:40.6, as was "officially" claimed, he had taken a ridiculous two minutes and twenty seconds to run the last 376 yards! There was no question that Desyatchikov had been conned into running an extra quarter of a mile.

Pyarnakivi had indeed run the correct distance, but he had been beaten at that distance by 24 seconds by Truex. Truex, however, had been gulled into running an extra lap by Ashenfelter's well-intentioned advice: Ashenfelter could not have foretold that his good suggestion would backfire. Even the experienced American referee, Pincus Sober, couldn't figure things out on the spot and so didn't register a protest at the time. By the next day he understood what had happened and lodged a claim, but the rules require that any protest must be submitted in writing within two hours after the completion of the day's meet. The Russians rejected the tardy argument that Truex was entitled to second place, and they were within their legal rights to do so. Apart from their clear legal justification, nothing about this race can ever be held up as gospel truth, anyway.

Track fanatic that I've been, I have seen, either in person or on television, all the great distance runners of my time right back to Paavo Nurmi. The roster is impressive: Emil Zatopek, Vladimir Kuts, Pyotr Bolotnikov, Gaston Roelants, Ron Clarke, Frank Shorter, Lasse Viren, and many others. I've seen them run in

Olympics and in wildly close and exciting record-breaking performances, but for the most part they are all blurred memories, along with, I must confess, the splendid but not particularly electrifying winner of this 10,000-meter race, Aleksey Desyatchikov.

But Bob Soth, Hubert Pyarnakivi, and Max Truex are fixed vividly in my memory forever.

CHAPTER 22

"What's a Dropkick, Grandpa?"

A question for archaeologists

"What's a dropkick, Grandpa?"

The question startled me for a moment, coming as it did from my grandson, Alex, who invariably seems to me to know as much about football as Don Shula or Joe Paterno. Whenever we have watched a game together on television, he's been the one who would explain to me the specialized roles played today in such modern positions on a professional football team as cornerbacks, linebackers, and tight ends. My own most intense interest in football was when the college game hogged all the headlines and a team was essentially 11 men plus a few substitutes who would get into the game for one reason or another. I had come to realize that for many years players had not been expected to play the entire game on both offense and defense and that now there was one platoon that confined its operations to defense and another complete platoon for offense. But that's about as far as I had gone in my modern football education, and while I continued to enjoy watching this new type of game, I didn't completely approve of it. Give me the old Brown team, which once played entire games with only 11 men and went undefeated!

Alex, however, was really a very sophisticated football spectator, and watching games on television with him alongside was the equivalent of graduate school. John Madden, using his graphic chalkboard, might be able to analyze a play better than Alex could explain it without props, but not much better. And here he was asking me what a dropkick was!

But almost immediately I realized that not only my grandson, but probably none of my children, whose ages range one side or the other of 30, had ever seen or even heard of a dropkick. Let's see. I rather think that it was the Gogolak brothers, Pete at Cornell and Charlie at Princeton, who killed off dropkicking by showing that the soccer-style placekick was the surest and most effective way to kick field goals and extra points, and that was in the early 1960's, more than 20 years ago. But before that, although straight-ahead, non-soccer-style placekicking was a frequent alternative, the dropkick was a standard way of trying to boot a football between the goalposts for a score, and there were good reasons.

"Alex," I said, "the dropkick is still a perfectly legal way to score, but no one tries it any more because it's a lot harder to learn than taking a sideswipe leg swing at a football that is caught and set into position by somebody else. Before the wave of European soccer players was brought into the United States by both college and professional teams, a placement kicker would line up a step or two right behind where the ball would be positioned, and then boot it with his toe straight ahead. Almost anyone can be taught to do that at least acceptably, but back then the idea of kicking soccer style with the side of the foot hadn't occurred to anyone, and a lot more placement kicks were missed than happens today.

"But when a team had a real dropkicker, they used him, and I'll tell you why." (The fine thing about having grandchildren is not limited to the universal feeling of gratification that one's lineage will be continued for yet another generation. Perhaps even better is the acquisition of a new audience that will listen with rapt attention to your tales of how things were in the Good Old Days. You once had such an audience in your own children but probably lost it when they reached their early teens. After that they may have continued to listen to you out of affection or courtesy, but the chances are that you corralled them much as the Ancient Mariner did the Wedding Guest.)

"First, Alex," I continued, "I'd better explain what a dropkick actually is . . . or was. The ball was snapped back to the kicker, who stood only about as far back as a passer in the shotgun position stands today. He caught it and took one quick step forward with his nonkicking leg at the same time he was dropping the ball, point downward, in front of his kicking leg. But he didn't kick it the way a punter does; he let it drop right to the ground, and just at the point where it did hit and started to rebound, but before it ever could, he'd boot it up toward the goalposts. A dropkick would soar quickly, end over end, over the opposing linesmen who were trying to block it. They practically never were able to, because with no extra man having to handle the ball and position it properly, and with the kicker getting the ball off only a fraction of a second after the snap from center, there just wasn't time. That's one of the reasons why having a good dropkicker was a real asset for a team. Another was that everybody got a thrill out of seeing a finely executed dropkick—it was a thing of grace and beauty. The placement kick today is about as dull an affair to watch as any in football, at least for me, but there was a timing and a flair to a dropkick that has few parallels in sport. A baseball player trapping a fiercely hit grounder that takes a hard bounce right at his feet, and then making the fast underhand throw to first base, might be another one. A tennis player not only handling but effectively putting away a half volley, where he has to meet the ball scant inches above the court, might be another. A dropkick was really lovely to see."

"But Grandpa," said Alex, "could a dropkicker kick the ball as far and as well as a good soccer-style placekicker does today?"

"Alex, all I can tell you is that dropkickers like Albie Booth of Yale, who was around in my own time at college, and Charlie Brickley of Harvard, who was a little before then but who kicked five or six goals in a game when it was necessary, were always making life miserable for my own college, Princeton. But come to think of it, the most fabulous of all dropkickers was long before my time; the legends about Pat O'Dea of Wisconsin would be almost unbelievable except that they're documented by on-the-spot newspaper reporting. He was Wisconsin's punter as well, and the very best of his day, but we're talking about dropkicking. O'Dea held the world's record with a 63-yard successful field goal against Northwestern, but what was remembered best about him was the way he could kick goals by executing a dropkick on the dead run— which was legal back then. That maneuver, with successful kicks throughout three seasons in lengths up to one 55-yarder, won many days for the University of Wisconsin over her Big Ten rivals."

I had finished my dissertation, and there was silence for a few seconds while Alex thought about it. Then he piped up again.

"Grandpa, what's the Statue of Liberty play?"

CHAPTER 23

Eternal Triangles

Willie Hoppe won 51 world titles over 47 years

The ticket taker at the door of the Grand Ballroom of the old Pennsylvania Hotel in New York City didn't know quite what to do about me that winter evening in 1922. I had a ticket all right, but this event was listed as a formal dress affair, and I believe I was the only nonconformist among all the eager spectators who had flocked to the hotel to see the world-championship sporting event that was being held there that night. The difficulty was that I didn't own a tuxedo and wouldn't even have been able to rent one my size. You see, I was 11 years old.

But I was accompanied by two properly attired young men in their twenties, my suit was a modest dark-blue serge, and I wore a black bow tie purchased especially for this occasion. After a moment's deliberation the ticket taker waved me in. Perhaps he didn't want to make a scene at this extremely elegant social as well as sporting occasion. Perhaps he had a small son of his own. Anyhow, my older brother, Fred, his friend, Walter, and I were all able to make our way to the seats, which were arranged especially for this event around a billiard table located in the center of the ballroom floor. We found three good places, some way back from the table but raised to a height where we had a good, unobstructed view.

What was the affair that drew a fanatical audience to the Penn-

152

sylvania Hotel that night? It was the final, decisive match of the 18.2 Balkline Billiards Championship of the world (the 18.2 designation will be explained shortly), and an intriguing human story lay behind it. It concerned a person whom an 11-year-old boy normally would not have known or cared about, he being more entranced by other idols of the Golden Age of Sport such as Babe Ruth, Jack Dempsey, Bill Tilden, and Bobby Jones, but I had been brainwashed into knowing and caring about Willie Hoppe, too. This is how it happened.

Walter's family and ours lived in the same Long Island town, and in those palmy days many more people than now lived in sumptuous houses with pretty lavish embellishments. Walter's home, for example, boasted a splendid oak-paneled billiard room with a table of the sort ordained for the aristocratic "gentleman's game" of carom billiards. Such a table has no pockets, and only three balls are used.

At that time pocket billiards—pool—although even then by far the more popular game nationally, had nothing like the prestige of billiards. It was even considered a little vulgar, since the poolroom was known as the hangout of youthful roughnecks. Times have changed, and attitudes with them. Pool is an excellent and eminently respected pastime today, even for "gentlemen," while billiards almost doesn't exist in this country anymore except in private clubs. Why? I suspect it's because anybody with modest skills can play some sort of pool and have satisfaction and fun, even if he is a rank amateur. Whereas billiards is an art, calling for both knowledge and a touch with the cue far more deft and complex that what is needed at the pool table. A casual pool player can make a decent run now and then, but a casual billiards player simply can't do that at all, even in the game's most simple form, straight rail. Straight rail comes down to executing a shot in which the player's cue ball caroms off one of the two object balls onto the other, which sounds simple. It isn't, if you're hoping to score more than one or two caroms.

Walter, who had the table in his house and could practice,

became a creditable amateur player after a while; he could often put together a run of 20 or 30. But Fred and I (even when I grew older than 11) never could achieve more than four or five caroms in a row, and that infrequently. Still, despite the ineptitude of two of us at even this most rudimentary form of billiards, we three became passionate fans of the game. The aura surrounding billiards was unique, and it was described most enchantingly in a short essay entitled *Eternal Triangles* by William Bolitho, which Walter had printed and framed elegantly to hang on one wall of his billiard room. (This title is so appropriate for what takes place in a game of billiards that I've latched on to it as the title for this chapter, with a grateful acknowledgment to Bolitho's ghost.)

Straight rail may have intrigued tyros like us, but it almost immediately became a bore for the billiard geniuses, of whom there were perhaps half a dozen in the world. They could gather the three balls into a corner within a very few shots at the beginning of a game, and then gently "nurse" them there, shot after shot, back and forth, the cue ball traveling no more than short inches, and the two object balls in the corner scarcely moving at all. If Fred or I—or you—tried to do that, the balls would come out of the corner and separate after a shot or two. But the master billiard artists could go on indefinitely, and that word is no exaggeration, for they rolled up hundreds and hundreds of caroms without ever missing, virtually keeping all three balls "under a hat." Something had to be done to elicit greater displays of skill from the experts and make the game more interesting for them and the spectators, and the invention of "balkline billiards" turned out to be the answer, with the game of 18.2 balkline eventually becoming the championship test.

There are four intersecting white lines on the green felt billiard tabletop, each being 18 inches away from a rail and parallel to it. This makes four square boxes, one at each corner, and four rectangular boxes, one along each rail. When both object balls (the red one and your opponent's cue ball) were gathered together in a box, they were said to be "in balk," and in 18.2 balkline you were allowed to execute only two caroms before having to drive at least one of the object balls out of the box. (Hence the name 18.2—in 18.1 you could only make one carom before having to separate the balls. After experimentation, it was decided that 18.2 was the better game.) If you were skillful enough to strike an object ball so that it came back on the same stroke or soon afterward, and to collect the three balls in a corner again so that you could click off two more easy caroms before having to drive a ball out of balk again, you were very, very good—though you might not be another Willie Hoppe.

Who was Willie Hoppe? Well, at the time of the Pennsylvania Hotel tournament he was 35 years old, but he had been known throughout the billiard world ever since he was about eight. Willie and his slightly older brother, Frank, were the sons of a barber who ran a combined barber shop-lunchroom in the town of Cornwall Landing, some 50 miles north of New York City. Father Hoppe's place was the town's social center, and a main attraction was the pool table (with pockets) alongside the lunchroom. Willie became fascinated with the game when he was five or six, and since he was too small to reach the height of the table, his grandfather fashioned a little wooden bench for him to stand on while making his shots. Even that wasn't high enough for little Willie to make many of the shots required, so he often executed those while lying flat on his stomach on top of a rail. Both Frank and Willie became expert pool players, and Father Hoppe augmented his weekly income substantially by betting on one of his sons against any visiting drummer who fancied his game. He was a good player himself, and his technique was to see to it that he just barely won a game by a very small margin and then, when asked for a return game, would proclaim that he had to attend to business adding, "I've got a couple of little kids who I'll bet can beat you!"

Frank was slightly the better shot at pool, because he was a couple of years older and tall enough to use his cue with the conventional, underhand stroke. Willie had to execute his shots sidearm, or even overhead, and in doing so he developed an incredibly soft delicate touch. The result was that the boys became famous locally and went on a state tour that included playing before the great Maurice Daly at his celebrated billiard parlor. Daly told Hoppe's father that Willie was born to play carom billiards and would be a genius at it. The Hoppes thereafter left pool to Frank, who soon wearied of being a child wonder on tour and turned to a more normal life. But Willie's special talent was nurtured, and he soon was a well-known national sports figure. In 1906, when he was 18, he won international fame in the world championship in Paris, where he soundly trimmed all rivals, including the hitherto invincible Maurice Vignaux of France. The game played at that tournament was 18.1 balkline, which up to then had been the championship game, but it was the last time, for 18.2 soon took over and remained the game for all future world championships.

From this point on, year after year, it was the world against Hoppe. Vignaux and the other great past masters, in particular Jacob (The Wizard) Schaefer, Sr., passed from the scene, and although several new marvelous performers sprang up, it wasn't until almost 15 years later that anyone really threatened Hoppe. The challenge came from, of all people, Jacob Schaefer's son, Young Jake Schaefer. In 1921 he finally took the 18.2 title away from Hoppe by tying him in the regular tournament and then beating him in a playoff. It was an upset comparable to Gene Tunney's later victory over Jack Dempsey, and interest among billiards fanatics was at fever pitch as to what would happen when Schaefer and Hoppe next met again in a championship match. That is why so many people, including our threesome, descended upon the Hotel Pennsylvania that November night in 1922.

Approximately a thousand seats had been set up in the ballroom, and space for several hundred people to stand had also been arranged; nevertheless, approximately 3,000 people had to be turned away. Walter had had the foresight to buy tickets the moment they became available, but outside the hotel speculators were hawking tickets for five to 10 times the admission price of three dollars. Apart from Hoppe and Schaefer, the four other greatest billiards players in the world were competing in this round-robin event: Welker Cochran of the United States, Edouard Horemans of Belgium, Eric Hagenlacher of Germany, and Roger Conti of France. In the course of a week, each contestant was scheduled to meet each of the other five once, the Schaefer-Hoppe contest to be the final one. That was the day for which Walter had secured our precious tickets. When it rolled around Hoppe had beaten all four of the men he had met so far, while Schaefer had won over Hagenlacher, Conti, and Cochran, but had lost to Horemans, who had lost twice. If Schaefer were to beat Hoppe they would be tied, as they had been the previous year, and would meet in another playoff for the title, but if Hoppe won, he would be undefeated and would regain his championship.

Without going into the details, suffice it to report that we three spectators hung breathlessly on every stroke, and in the end, Willie Hoppe, with an unfinished run of 106, scored his 500th point while Schaefer had achieved only 283. Willie was world champion again, to our intense delight. It wasn't that we had anything against Young Jake Schaefer or the others—they were all marvels commanding nothing but admiration—but Hoppe was above admiration, he was an idol. (In one 18.2 balkline exhibition he ran 622 points, a mark that wasn't broken for 20 years.)

That 1922 championship was one of the 51 world titles that Willie Hoppe won in the years between 1906 and 1952, when at the age of 65 he finally retired. No sports champion in history ever had so long and successful a reign, and he acheived it despite changing games in midcareer. For Hoppe's dominance at 18.2 balkline became shaky as he approached 40 years of age and younger men like Jake Schaefer, Jr., were taking over. The exquisitely deft touch with a cue fades a bit with age, and Hoppe actually contemplated retiring when a few years passed and he no longer was winning the championships, even though he still was coming close. But then, in the early 1930's, he turned to that other magnificent billiards game that is played on a table with no pockets, three-cushion billiards, and started specializing in that. The rest is heartwarming sports history.

In three-cushion billiards the cue ball has to strike at least three sides of the table before completing the carom onto the second object ball. Obviously, this is infinitely harder to achieve than a straight carom, requiring a profound grasp of geometry as well as skill; a really long run such as masters make regularly, even at balkline, is out of the question. Hoppe still holds the record high run in a scheduled match game—20 points—which is just as impressive as his runs of hundreds of points at balkline. His three-cushion career is even more remarkable than his balkline one, for from 1936 on he won *every* world championship tournament that was held, until, after winning the 1952 event, he decided to retire.

How did it happen that Hoppe, no longer quite as good at balkline as he had been when younger, could then become the very greatest at a more complex game? The infinite delicacy of stroke that characterizes a balkline master's genius is only one part of what's required to be brilliant at three-cushion, and Hoppe possessed the other parts to a degree that no one else has ever rivaled: the ability to shoot with unerring straightness, and a knowledge of all the angles formed by a ball as it strikes at least three rails before completing its journey to the second object ball. Eternal triangles or even more involved geometric figures: no one could compare with Willie Hoppe in visualizing them.

When Hoppe finally decided to lay down his competitive cue, he was still as good as ever, but he must have felt that he had nothing more to prove, and that 65 was a fitting retirement age. He went to live in Miami, where he gave regular exhibitions right up to his death, at age 71, on February 1, 1959. I made a point of going to see one once, and Willie was as marvelous as ever, still decked out in a tuxedo and bow tie. Even though the great popularity of billiards had declined a lot by the time of his death, Hoppe's obituary was a Page One feature in the *New York Times* and ran over, with photographs of the man at various ages, into another full column about his career on an inside page. He was the only billiards player ever asked to give an exhibition at the White House, which he did at William Howard Taft's request in 1911. One of his greatest victories came in the three-cushion championship in 1940, where he was pitted twice against each of the other top players in the world and won all 20 games. That was a feat unparalleled in billiards history, but Hoppe did almost as well the following year, when he was hospitalized with a fever of 106° on the day the tournament started. Play was well under way a couple of days later when, still running a low fever, he persuaded his doctor to release him. He caught up with the tournament by playing extra matches each day; in an 18-man field, where he had to encounter each of the other 17 once, he won every match except one. That was more than sufficient for him to retain his title.

Willie Hoppe must have been a physical marvel. You may not think that billiards requires much in the way of athletic condition, but Hoppe's career wasn't at all like an evening's casual game at the club. For approximately half a century the sort of magic that Hoppe wielded with his cue demanded stamina, nerve control, and deftness of hand past any other type of sport. To find something that might compare with it, you might name brain surgery, but brain surgeons don't keep at it steadily for 50 years. Hoppe was still beating the top billiards players in the world when he was in his sixties, consistently beating young experts who were not born when he first became world champion. In the sport of eternal triangles, Hoppe himself seemed eternal.

CHAPTER 24

The Little Red Notebook

*How clerical aptitude can keep your
tennis game going*

Every January 1 for a great many years I've made sure that I had a new, leather-bound appointment book for the coming year small enough to be tucked into the outside breast pocket of a jacket. Sometimes it was black, sometimes red or blue, but they all had one feature that was of at least equal significance to me as the book's basic function of providing spaces for jotting down dates and times and making small notes and memoranda. That feature is the section headed "Addresses and Telephone Numbers."

It's not that I have such a wide circle of friends, relatives, or business associates whose vital statistics I must carry around with me. Even in my more gadabout days this section didn't get much of a workout, consisting in the main of names, addresses, and telephone numbers of young women, and I didn't know very many. Surely I knew all their names, and probably their addresses and telephone numbers, by heart, and I only filled in a list in my little book to give myself some feeling of importance. So the list was virtually of no use to me, and it certainly wasn't to anybody else. I don't think anyone ever called me up to ask if I could fix him up with a date.

I still latch onto a small book of this sort each New Year—a red one this year—but now the "Addresses and Telephone Numbers" section has taken over completely. It is so jam-packed with pertinent information about tennis players I know, and new ones I keep running into, that it has to be extended onto the pages that are intended to be used for recording your business expenses, or your wife's glove size. If I record a woman's name on that list, it's because she's a good tennis player and would fit into our game with no reservations. I started with an original cadre of perhaps a couple of dozen good club players I knew in the New York City area, and each time I meet a new, promising candidate for the list, I add his (or her, and let's agree that from now on "his" means "his or her") name to the roster. I now have over 80 names, with pertinent notes about those I've only encountered once or twice. Also, each summer we vacation for a period of time somewhere, usually in Connecticut or Long Island, and fairly often in England. They are all places we go back to, so I've built up comparable, if smaller, dossiers for each location.

The fact is that I go past the simple notation of a person's name, address, and telephone number. Primarily I note what the level of his game appears to be, which is best determined, of course, by playing with him. Failing that, with first encounters a few minutes' chat about the level of play a person actually has attained, or even thinks he has, can place him reasonably well. For brevity's sake I use the National Tennis Rating Program figures to make my notations. This is a self-evaluation system for the most part, ranging from a 1.0 rating for a beginner to a 7.0 rating for a nationally high-ranked player. Good to excellent club players usually fall in the 4.0 to 5.5 range. All of the players on my list are of that calibre, with the majority around 4.5, and the best of us is perhaps 5.0. We wouldn't be embarrassed if by chance a 5.5 player should join our game, but he'd dominate it. Conversely, a player who was no better than a 3.5 would not have a happy time trying to keep up with the solid club level of our group. Years ago, when I was much younger and could really cover a singles court effectively, I think I would have been rated a 5.0 player. Today I've really given up singles, but as a doubles player, with only my half of the court to be responsible for, I think I'm still at least a 4.5. That's about in the middle of the doubles games I play in every week, but my passion for playing is second to no one.

As I grew older and the new people I met inevitably turned out to be younger, I came to the conclusion that if I wanted to be sure of regular quality games, it would be wise to make myself a fountainhead of information about players, their competence, and their availability. Except in the case of established regular games of old doubles friends, most people are inclined to wait until called, and not try to get up a game themselves if it's at all difficult. I've built up my little book to a point where I'd try to copyright it if it didn't have to be revised and updated so frequently.

We have one game throughout the winter where we have two courts for two hours each, side by side, and we switch partners and opponents after each set. I not only have been able to see to it that the requisite eight players were on hand each week, but also usually have wistful people dropping hints that they'd like to be invited in, this week or next week or *some* week. We have a pretty solid bunch of eight players who get first call, but usually one or two of them can't make it for one reason or another, and that's when I spring into action with my little red book. Once I have our eight signed up, I also draw up a kind of "dance program" of the pairings for each of the three sets we invariably play in two hours, so we don't waste any precious playing time discussing it.

This has been going on for some 20 years, and I've never come up empty and failed to fill the game. It's been close sometimes, on occasions like a long major holiday weekend when people go out of town, but I've always come through in the end. My list is so well-known that I've had relative strangers telephone me to say that they were running a tournament and needed, let us say, four more players to fill out the draw sheet, and could I suggest a few who might be interested?

Certain other footnotes contain helpful information on my list. How available is a working person other than weekends? Has he a car, should choice or necessity (which is often the case) have determined that the game site be some distance away? There are times when a 4.0 player with a car is preferable to a 5.0 player who has only a subway token. I add no footnotes about character or agreeableness. There's no point in confusing issues for passionate tennis players, whose goal is to be sure there's a game. If the day comes when the level of Jimmy Connors's or John McEnroe's game declines to about 5.0 or lower, there won't be any argument about asking them in, despite their frequently lamentable tennis manners. If we were only able to round up seven players, Attila the Hun would be welcome as the eighth, assuming that he could keep a rally going for at least a few strokes.

CHAPTER 25

The One and Only Absolute Best

The all-time sports champion without any argument

It's been almost 60 years since I attended my first Millrose Games indoor track meet as the manager of my school track team, and I've been hooked ever since. After I stopped getting in free as a college manager, I bought two of the best loge seats in the house (which was then the old Madison Square Garden) and have attended every year since, with the exception of the World War II years, when I was overseas. The Millrose people kept my reservation intact while I was in the Army and, when the new Garden was built, issued me comparably good seats. For some years my wife, Toni, went with me, until she no longer felt she had to pretend she liked attending that much. In recent years it's been one of my two sons. I take Greg in even-numbered years because there are four letters in his name and Roger in the odd years. We can remember whose turn it is that way.

The buildup for the February 1986 Millrose Games involved more speculation and anticipation than I could remember since the memorable old days when the rivalry in the mile run was always the star attraction. In the space of just a little more than six weeks preceding the 1986 meet, the indoor world record in the pole vault had been broken seven times—and by three different men! Billy Olsen of the United States had started things off with a leap of 19'2¾" just before the beginning of the year, and two weeks later Sergei Bubka, the Russian holder of the outdoor record, topped that by a quarter of an inch. Two days later Billy Olsen soared another quarter of an inch higher than that, and a week later went even higher, an additional half inch this time, to bring the record to 19'3¾". One week later a completely unexpected performance took place when a relatively unknown American vaulter named Joe Dial added another inch to the record. That height stood for exactly one more week until Bubka vaulted 19'5" for a new record; just hours later on the same day but thousands of miles away, Olsen reclaimed the record with a leap of 19'5½".

Now, six days later, all three men would meet for the first time, and the frenetic expectations of Howard Schmertz, who runs the Millrose Games, and the sportswriters were matched only by Greg's and mine. It was Greg's turn, remember—an even year, 1986. Roger was wistful, but as things turned out he had no need to be. The meet was plagued by bad fortune all the way, and the much heralded pole vault turned out to be almost an utter dud. Olsen and a long shot, Dave Volz, did clear 19 feet, which is not to be sneezed at, but in view of the buildup, the event was distinctly disappointing, and this was particularly so because both Olsen and Dial were granted an extra vault each when it seemed that both had been eliminated. The justification given was that photographers had interfered with their runs, but I would bet my shirt that if a new record had been set as a result of this leniency, it would have been thrown out by the international federation. At the time Bubka protested so strongly that the event was held up for almost an hour while the diplomats tried to avert a Cold War USA-USSR confrontation. It was finally resolved by giving Bubka, who had also failed to clear the bar at this lower height on any of his legitimate three tries, an extra attempt like the others. Bubka missed that, too, so both he and Dial were complete washouts after all the hoopla, neither placing even in the top five, and though Olsen and the incidental nearest thing to a hero, Volz, did achieve the respectable 19-foot level, the entire event, like much of the meet, was tainted. Official blunder after blunder took place, and the 1986 Millrose Games must surely have been the worst-conducted meet in indoor track history. Roger probably was lucky that his name has five letters in it and he goes in odd years.

All of this is just the preliminary to what I discussed with Greg on the way home, which was the history of a certain pole-vaulter of the past who, in my opinion, was the only athlete in any sport who could really and convincingly be considered the greatest of all time in his sport—in a class by himself.

It's always fun in any sport to compare one generation's heroes with another generation's idol. Who was better, Jack Dempsey or Muhammad Ali? Walter Johnson or Sandy Koufax? Bill Tilden or Don Budge? Bobby Jones or Jack Nicklaus? Babe Ruth or Joe DiMaggio? Such discussions make for splendid locker-room chatter, but even the most persuasive and fanatical debater cannot emerge from such arguments as the clear winner.

Circumstances and conditions change too much from one era to another for any athlete, no matter how great, to be rated the best of all time in his or her field. Paavo Nurmi's fastest time for the mile run was some 20 seconds slower than those Sebastian Coe and Steve Ovett and Steve Cram and others run regularly now, but if they all were contemporaries, does anyone really believe that Nurmi would be left struggling 150 yards or more behind the rest? Comparisons like these are absurd because they're based upon unexamined evidence. The best an athlete can be is the best of his era.

With one exception.

Cornelius (Dutch) Warmerdam was not only without question the world's best pole-vaulter over a stretch of about a decade, from the late 1930's to the mid 1940's, but he was also clearly the best athlete in his sport who ever lived, and this is the one such argument about comparative bests that I'd be willing to take to the Supreme Court.

Greg seemed a little dubious about so sweeeping a statement, and with the astute rebuttal skill that led him to pursue a legal career, said, "What about Bob Beamon's 29'2¼" long jump in the 1968 Olympics, which cracked the then existing record by almost two feet and has never been equaled since?" I had to agree that Beamon's feat was outstanding, but it was accomplished in the rarified atmosphere of Mexico City's high altitude. Furthermore, it also could be considered even more of a once-in-a-lifetime freak miracle than a golfer's hole-in-one. Beamon never again came close to achieving that distance again. But before presenting the case for Warmerdam and his unique record, I told Greg that I'd like to indulge in a little digression about athletic performance (not that he really needed it, but perhaps you, the reader, are not as steeped in sports history as any child of mine—and now, God help them— grandchild of mine is likely to be).

Of all sports, track and field is one of the most measurable in that times and distances are accurately taken. But changes in both psychological and physical conditions make realistic comparisons among champions whose careers were separated by many years practically impossible. The main psychological aspect is that once a hitherto and supposedly unattainable feat has been accomplished by one athlete, others know it can be done, and almost imme- diately they, too, do it. Not even the best great distance runners could break the four-minute-mile barrier until Roger Bannister finally achieved it. Almost immediately, however, John Landy repeated the feat, and since then it has become commonplace. Hundreds of sub-four-minute miles have been run, and today a championship mile that's clocked right around four minutes flat is regarded as slow.

The physical changes that make comparisons between different generations pointless are more obvious. In track, there are things like better running surfaces and completely new and much more arduous training programs and coaching techniques. In the field, completely new events have evolved from old ones as the result of innovations either in techniques, as in the case of the 180-degree turn in the shot put and the Fosbury flop in the high jump, or in equipment, such as the fiberglass pole in the vault, which made an instant mockery of old records. Nevertheless, the psychological principle outlined above has held true: when a track or field record is set under new conditions, it is immediately equaled or beaten by rivals, and only minuscule gaps exist between the best performances and the next-best. Beamon's long jump seems to be an exception, but as I had pointed out to Greg, one swallow does not a summer make, and one marvelous long jump does not make the jumper the best who ever lived. Cornelius Warmerdam, on the other hand, didn't just outvault his rivals by the equivalent of a country mile on one or a few occasions; he did it all the time for years. Let's look at the record.

Dutch Warmerdam was a very good but not extraordinary college pole-vaulter throughout most of his career at Fresno State in the mid-1930's. Those were the days of the bamboo pole, and Warmerdam was a consistent 13'6" to 14-foot vaulter, which was good enough to win him more than his share of college events, but not to attract much national attention. That attention first came his way in his final year at Fresno State, in 1937, when he suddenly started to vault really competitively against the two best in the world at that time, Earle Meadows, the 1936 Olympic champion, and Bill Sefton, who was just about as good as Meadows. All three cleared 14'7⅝" that year. Sefton and Meadows actually approached 15 feet and set a new world record when each vaulted 14'11", but neither ever came that close again.

Warmerdam kept on vaulting after college and reached his full development from 1940 through the middle of the decade, when he was in his late twenties. In the first of those years he cleared the bar at 15'1", and so became the first 15-foot vaulter in history. No one else topped that height for more than 10 years, and when it finally was accomplished by a second man, the U.S.'s Reverend Bob Richards, it wasn't done with the old bamboo pole that Warmerdam always used but with the new metal pole that gave vaulters a decided step upward. Nor did Richards set any new record, because meanwhile, in those early years of the 1940's, Warmerdam had vaulted better than 15 feet a total of 43 times, culminating his spectacular undefeated and unrivaled streak when he set an outdoor record of 15'7³/4" and an indoor one of 15'8¹/2" before retiring from competition. These were the World War II years, and Dutch was an ensign and a Navy lieutenant for much of the time. Because of the war the 1940 and 1944 Olympics were canceled, so he never had the chance to win the gold medals that surely would have been his, but his place in track history doesn't require that at all. His outdoor record stood for 15 years and his indoor mark for 16 years. When Bob Gutowski bettered the former, and Don Bragg the latter, the margin of victory was less than an inch—and they did it with metal poles.

No other athlete in all sports history has been so far better than the next-best, and over such a length of time. Warmerdam was consistently a foot or a foot and a half better than his nearest rivals in an event where the margin is usually no more than a couple of inches. After he retired in 1947, it was as if the clock had suddenly been set back in the pole-vault event: men vaulting 13'6" and 14 feet were winning national championships again.

In the first Olympics held after the war, in 1948 in London, the winning height was 14'1¹/4", and the silver medalist cleared 13'9¹/4". Four years later at Helsinki and eight years later at Melbourne, Richard's winning heights still fell short of the 15-foot mark, considerably lower than what Warmerdam had achieved 43 times over the previous dozen years! No wonder an old Olympic medalist, Nat Carmell, said of him that "he was the only all-time, indisputable, supreme champion the athletic world has ever known."

In the 1960's the fiberglass pole took over from the metal pole and all past records went out the window. Fiberglass introduced new factors into the mechanics of the event that enabled vaulters to be catapulted to glorious new heights far above anything they could ever aspire to reach with the metal pole. Immediately, a new crop of catapulters made a shambles of the Warmerdam records—

over 16 feet in 1962, 17 feet in 1963, and then, despite a slowing of the bar's inexorable ascent, 18 feet in 1970 and 19 feet in the 1980's. Twenty feet seems so sure to be attained fairly soon that it may well happen before this book is published. More power to this new breed, but unless and until another superman like Dutch Warmerdam comes along, there isn't a vaulter who can be mentioned in the same breath.

Who was better, Ted Williams or Willie Mays? Jim Thorpe or Red Grange? Man O'War or Citation? Rod Laver or Bjorn Borg? Ben Hogan or Tom Watson? Sugar Ray Robinson or Sugar Ray Leonard?

I don't know. All I'm sure about is who was the best.

CHAPTER 26

Color My Eyeglasses Rosy

Some modest proposals about rules

Diehards in sport like things the way they are, whereas radicals are always trying to change the rules. In past years the traditionalist in me has sympathized with the diehards, but in recent times certain innovative ideas have made sense often enough for me to have become something of a diesoft. Not only have I refrained from stubbornly insisting that rules are rules and damn well ought to be left alone, but I actually have come up with a few radical suggestions of my own.

Take football. I must admit that I was upset some years ago when college football did away with the tradition of allowing only one extra point after a touchdown and introduced the option of running, or passing the ball over the goal line for two points. It has turned out to be a most attractive feature of the college game, and one that adds a spark of imagination and daring to a sport often sadly lacking in those qualities, since playing the percentages is generally a coach's guiding principle. That innovation has yet to be adopted in professional football, which year after year has steadfastly refused to adopt the two-point option, despite its obvious advantages, which are even greater for the professional game than they are for the college one.

Tie games, which now require the essentially unfair sudden-death overtime period, would virtually be eliminated, as they have been in college contests. James Graham, Marquess of Montrose, once wrote:

> He either fears his fate too much,
> Or his deserts are small,
> That puts it not unto the touch,
> To win or lose it all.

College coaches have invariably—and properly—made the decision not to risk Graham's contempt: given the choice of tying a game with a one-point kick conversion or winning it with a successful two-point pass or run, they have elected to risk the latter. I'm confident that if the professional rules actually were changed so that the two-point option was available, professional coaches would be forced to do the same. But the rule may never be changed, because the coaches would have to vote it in, and professional coaches are frightened at the prospect. They don't want to be forced to be daring now and then, and to take the criticism if their daring doesn't work out. They'd rather lose unimaginatively and be comforted by the thought that they couldn't be criticized because they "played the percentages."

What happens when a coach chooses to kick the extra point that ties a professional game? It goes into sudden-death overtime, which I termed "essentially unfair" a few sentences back. That's because the team that wins the flip of a coin at that stage always chooses to receive, and does so quite understandably. All they need do is to run off enough yardage to give a good placement kicker a decent shot at winning the game without the other team's ever getting the ball! Sudden-death overtimes, therefore, are often won as the direct result of calling the flip of a coin correctly. So I'm against sudden-death, and it would virtually disappear in professional football if the two-point option were adopted. Also, what a boon it would be to the all-important television producers to know that a game would definitely be over by such and such an hour and wouldn't drag on, because of overtime, into prime time scheduling!

Still, if we're stuck with sudden-death overtime in the pro game, as I imagine we will continue to be, I have a few suggestions to make it fairer, on the one hand, and more interesting, on the other. In the interest of fairness, decree that a team has to win by six points—by a touchdown or *two* field goals. (Send that man to his room who protests that three safeties will do it, too!) Six points would require the receiving team to drive the length of the field and cross the goal line in order to win—or else kick a comparatively easy field goal, hold the other team, and when they get the ball again manage to get sufficiently close to kick *another* field goal. This much harder but much fairer procedure admittedly has the drawback that it would take even longer, but once a major TV network has preempted a portion of a scheduled show, it might as well preempt a bit more.

Sticking to the sad acceptance of the idea that the two-point conversion will be voted down indefinitely by the pros, might we not change some things about the extra point that would jazz it up, and even act to eliminate tie games and overtimes in many cases? How would it be if bonus points were given to the kicking team if it chose to make its extra-point try a more difficult one? What if a team lined up, let us say, on the 20-yard line, so that the kicker had to make it good from something like 37 yards. That's a lot harder than the almost assured result of the inevitably successful chip shot that follows touchdowns now. It ought to be worth *two* points, let's say, and that extra point could make the difference in a close game in the same fashion as the two-point option does in college circles. Then we might have the option of adding on another 15 yards, the lineup taking place on the 35-yard line and the kick having to be better than 50 yards. A successful effort at that distance would be worth *three* points. I suspect that teams with good placekickers might well choose to exercise the privilege of trying for more than one point after a touchdown even quite early in a game, and not just near the end of one, when the game's result depends on it. This idea would make the specialist placekicker infinitely more important than he is now, but would that be a bad thing? After all, the game is called *foot*ball.

Baseball rules are pretty solid and don't change much over the years, which is one of the reasons why it's so beloved a sport of so many. The one important rule change in modern times has been the adoption of the designated hitter by the American League. Since the National League has not gone along with the concept, and there are good arguments both for and against, I'm not going to enter this particular debate except to hope that one day soon the two leagues will agree, one way or the other. As things now stand, injustices are worked at the time of the World Series, when a team from one league has to accommodate itself to the rules of the other league in a critical game.

My only thought about a change in baseball rules has to do with the intentional base on balls, the dullest thing in the game. We don't want to do away with it, though, because it's a legitimate stratagem, nor do we want to make it automatic, waving the batter to first base without a pitch being thrown. But why not liven things up a little by permitting the batter to step across the plate and swing at the ball? He'd have to wait until the pitcher released the ball before he could leave the batter's box, but since the catcher is allowed to leave the confines of the box, why shouldn't the batter too? The possibility exists that the pitcher might cross him up with an honest hard one across the plate, which could hit a too-eager hitter. So you wouldn't want to venture out of the box unless you felt sure the pitch was going wide of the plate. If you made a mistake and got plunked in the ribs, you would lose. You wouldn't get to take first base, and the pitch would be called a strike.

If this simple rule change were instituted, the pitcher would have to throw the ball so wide of the plate that the batter would have virtually no chance to reach it, or else he'd put more mustard on the ball than on the conventional lob used today, or both. Any of these variations could lead to a wild pitch or a passed ball, and because there is invariably a man, or two, on base in this situation, it would be a very important wild pitch or passed ball. But let the pitcher throw closer, and there would be the batter, ready to scurry across and reach out and smack the ball. The dullest moments in baseball could change to ones in which everybody would be waiting to see what might happen.

Now tennis. Here's a sport in which what was considered a radical new rule has worked out splendidly. When Jimmy Van Alen first proposed his sudden-death scoring plan, we traditionalists were against it. But gradually all of us began to recognize how attractive it is. The fact that Van Alen's original sudden-death idea has been superseded by the slightly less drastic "lingering-death" system isn't important. The basic change was good. The rule has helped everyone—stars, television, administrators, and all of us recreational players whose court time may be limited and who want to settle the outcome of a set before time runs out.

I have a minor suggestion for a change in tennis, far less radical than Van Alen's and far less important but, I think, eminently sensible. Under present rules a let ball is in play at all times, except on the serve. A let ball during play generates unusual excitement, requiring quick reactions if it's handled successfully. If it's legal at all other times, why should it not be on the serve too? It would add an occasional delicious note of uncertainty, possibly benefiting the server or, equally possibly, the receiver. Moreover, it would do away with the absurd judge who sits at midcourtside for hours, fingers on the net, waiting for the quiver that signals that a serve ticked the net in passing.

The only suggestion I would have for golf is not a practical one, the world and television finances being what they are. It's deplorable that the one event of the four major championships that constitute the Grand Slam, the PGA, had to forsake the match-play format that distinguished it from the other three tournaments, for there's something very special about match play that transcends even exciting medal play. Until 1958 the PGA was match play, and old-timers wouldn't trade memories of the man-to-man tussles between Walter Hagen and Gene Sarazen, or Byron Nelson and Sam Snead, or Snead and Ben Hogan for all the par-breaking medal rounds ever played in the PGA since then. But match play doesn't lend itself to the demands of major television, because top name players may be eliminated in an early round, and because there's no telling when a match will end. If it were to be a full round of 18 holes, the time it would take could be gauged accurately enough. But if Player A happened to beat Player B, four up and three to play, closing out the match on the 15th green, the network would be stuck with perhaps three quarters of an hour of expensive slot time to fill, and if they filled it with two-reelers of the Three Stooges comedies, how many major sponsors would step in to foot the bill? And so ended the one match-play major championship, more's the pity. The only opportunity to savor it today to some extent, is the annual Skins Game gimmick, which I wrote about in the chapter about Jack Nicklaus, but that's no championship. It can be fascinating, but it remains a television gimmick.

Basketball is exciting as it stands, and on the whole, rule changes improved the game. The 24-second clock in the professional game has worked without complaint for a long time, and it has led to all the colleges adopting some sort of clock—either 30 or 45 seconds—which is all to the good. The three-point basket seems to be accepted in NBA circles, and it does add some zest in the closing minutes of a tight game, but on the whole I suspect that basketball could do nicely without it. Still, as it is played in the NBA, where the shot has to be taken from a distance that makes it considerably more likely to be missed than made, I am not opposed to it. Where it has gone a bit sour is in the college game, the flaw being that the designated distance of 19'9" is too easy for the sharpshooters: they are able to sink over 50 percent of their tries. That really upsets the balance of the game, and it is too severe a handicap for a team that may have played a much sounder and better game the length of the court throughout, only to lose on two or three consecutive three-pointers at the very end. Adding a couple of feet to the shot would probably rectify things, and with the almost unanimous condemnation of the college coaches during the first season of experimentation, I've little doubt that either the three-pointer will be eliminated or, as is more probable, the range extended.

Basketball players have grown about a foot taller than they used to be, and there are continual suggestions that the basket should be raised to make the stuff shot impossible, or at least a lot harder. There are good arguments pro and con, but the task of raising baskets on thousands of courts is too staggering to be contemplated by me. The same in a reverse way is true of ice hockey, where *more* scoring might benefit the game. There doesn't seem to be any easy way to encourage more scoring, other than to make the cage wider or higher, and life is hard enough for a goalie already.

Soccer, also, is too low scoring as a rule for American tastes. But purists have been bruised enough by changes made in the U.S. professional game, notably the "shootout," the one-on-one situation devised to settle matters if a game remains tied after two overtime periods. Players and coaches don't much like the shootout, but it's a clever conception, and soccer crowds seem to love it.

The fewer rules a game has, the better it is likely to be. (Baseball is an exception, and so is golf, which, although basically the simplest of sports, has an enormous code of regulations.) The most exciting team sport in the world may be Irish hurling, which often seems to have no rules at all. All you really need to have is a grasp of the scoring principles (three points for a ball hit under the crossbar of the H-shaped goalpost, one point for a ball hit over it), and a tolerant attitude toward potential mayhem and manslaughter. Yet despite the hard ball and the ax-handle sticks that flail away, the players come through remarkably unscathed, the game keeps moving without the interminable timeouts of American football, scoring is refreshingly high, the action volatile, and, faith, it's a grand sport entirely! I wish I had a chance to see it more often.

Well, I have wished for a number of changes here that might make sports more enjoyable to play and to watch. Right or wrong, the urge to tamper with matters beyond one's control goes a long way back—at least as far back as Omar Khayyám, who wrote in his *Rubaiyat*:

> Ah love! could you and I with Him conspire
> To grasp this sorry Scheme of Things entire,
> Would not we shatter it to bits—and then
> Re-mould it nearer to the Heart's desire!

CHAPTER 27

Veteran's Vaudeville

A man can dream, can't he?

Many, many years ago, when I was a teenager and, it would seem from the following, a pretty dewy-eyed one, I read a passage from an extremely saccharine novel that impressed my romantic instincts enough so that I read it aloud to my considerably older brother and his friend, who happened to be in the room. It would take a good deal of inane research now to dig up a copy of A. A. Milne's *Two People*, and I have no intention of undertaking it. I remember the general idea in the passage well enough, as set down in cold type by the whimsical creator of Winnie the Pooh. He had one of the characters in the novel pontificate that if a person could dictate an ideal life, it would be to be a famous athlete from the age of 15 to 25; a beautiful woman from 25 to 35; a dashing explorer-adventurer from 35 to 45; a world-famous writer from 45 to 55; a distinguished statesman from 55 to 65; and a *gardener* from 65 to 75.

I'm sure I haven't got it just right after all these years, but that's close enough. Anyhow, I read the passage aloud in a hushed and reverent voice. There was a moment's silence, and then my brother's friend commented mildly, "It seems to me that there'd be more kick in it to be a famous athlete from sixty-five to seventy-five!"

At the time I had to admit that he was right, and when I actually turned 65 he seemed more right than ever. I didn't have a wish in the world to be a gardener, for any of my pathetic efforts in the past had done nothing to earn me even the sobriquet of Pale Green Thumb Schwed. I imagine I am the only person in the Western Hemisphere who ever failed in the attempt to grow a privet hedge. It is virtually impossible, but I did it. I wanted no more of floriculture.

But hey there! How about really having a try at becoming a famous athlete at 65? After all, as a tennis player I've always been more than a respectable hacker.

Quickly I rummaged through a bureau drawer and dug out a copy of the United States Tennis Association's sanctioned tournaments, which are listed in a booklet twice a year. Was anything scheduled for my age bracket that I could reach easily while still holding down a New York City office job? There, lo and behold, I read that in early March the New York State Senior Indoor Championships for 45's, 55's, 60's, *and 65's*, would be held at the Parade Grounds Tennis Center in Brooklyn. Entry fee and application must be received by March. Eureka! It was still early January and I had time not only to file an entry but also to write a letter to see if it made any sense at all, or if I had rocks in my head.

The tournament was being conducted by Len Hartman, who owned the Parade Grounds courts and had long been a prestigious figure in metropolitan tennis circles. I pulled out my trusty typewriter and dashed off the following letter:

Dear Mr. Hartman,

We do not know each other, but we do have mutual friends. Apart from that, you may possibly recognize my name as being Allison Danzig's co-editor for the book *The Fireside Book of Tennis*. Additionally, I am the author of two of the first six books published by Doubleday as the USTA Instructional Series: *Sinister Tennis* (*How to Play Against and With*

Left-Handers), and the recent *The Serve and the Overhead Smash*. These books are by club-level players, and addressed to club-level players.

So much by way of introduction, but considering the purpose of this letter, it would perhaps be more to the point to define myself as a tennis player, a little more specifically than merely stating I am a pretty good club player. For I will be 66 a week from now, and so, on that basis, I am eligible for your Senior 65's tournament, but I'd appreciate learning from you whether I'm qualified as far as competence is concerned.

How good am I? In the autobiography I supplied for jacket copy on *The Fireside Book of Tennis*, I described myself as a player "of considerable local reputation so long as the local scene was no larger than about one square mile." As the editor/publisher both for Bill Tilden's last book, and for Rod Laver's book, I can boast of having faced each from the other side of the net without having been hospitalized, but I am quick to point out that these were doubles matches and that neither author wanted to see his publisher invalided, at least not until his book was published and safely in the bookstores.

As a rule, I play no more than a couple of hours twice, or perhaps three, times a week, and these days much more doubles than singles. But I can still be seduced into the latter and perform with some degree of success. In my summer community, where I once was the Number 1 player years ago, I still play on the town team that competes against neighboring community and club teams, and do well. Also, in round-robin doubles tournaments in the last couple of years, I was a winner at the tennis writers event that's held at the West Side Tennis Club at the time of each U.S. Open, and followed up by being one-half of the winning doubles team at the tournament for writers and celebrities, which was held in conjunction with the opening of the Bronx-Whitestone tennis complex. Finally, I did the same last year at the Association of American Publishers event at Boca Raton.

Is that degree of competence enough to get me into a real, sanctioned tournament, such as yours, and even if it is, am I likely to make a spectacle of myself? Would I be more realistic to go down to Florida and pitch horseshoes?

Sincerely yours,
Peter Schwed

A few days later, back came an application blank along with a scribbled note. Mr. Hartman was a man of considerably fewer words than I:

Dear Peter,

How good are you? Enter and find out! From your letter I would guess at least as good as some.

Len Hartman

The die was cast: I was going to do it. I had a couple of good reasons to do so, as I saw it. It would be fun and would make an unusual gambit for some future dinner-table conversations, and I might be able to write an amusing article, or chapter in a book, about it. From here on in I think I can best describe what happened in diary form.

January 21, 1977
Playing in any sanctioned tournament requires one to be a member of the United States Tennis Association, which isn't a hard thing to be elected to, as long as you have the requisite eight dollars and a stamped envelope. I sent in my application when I first thought of embarking upon this crusade, and so I already have my plastic card, quite as impressive as the American Express card, stating that I am a member in good standing of the USTA. On the back, in addition to such data as my identification number, is the date of my birth, January 18, 1911, which would be evidence that I qualify as

being eligible to play in a 65-and-over tournament. But the USTA didn't ask for a birth certificate, or anything like that, simply taking my word for it. I don't want to be too cynical in an already cynical world, but remembering the intensity of some of the veteran players I've run up against on New York City public courts—particularly at the old Rip's courts in Manhattan, where excellent and canny players smoked cigars while playing and had sizable bets on every match and smaller bets on every point—I can't help but wonder. There are a lot of pot-hunters—people who will do almost anything to win a trophy—in the tennis world. Could there possibly be white-haired 55-year-olds who claim to be 65 on their applications? Shame on you, Schwed, for even having the thought cross your mind!

January 25
I have filed my application and have sent the form, plus a twenty-buck entry fee, to Len Hartman. If I get bumped out of this tournament 6–0, 6–0 in the first round in half an hour, this is going to be one of the most expensive tennis dates I ever had. Oh well, easy come, easy go. It reminds me, to a much lesser degree, of the time when three of my four children were all attending Riverdale Country School at the same time, and parents were allowed to use the school's tennis courts on weekends during vacation. I used to proclaim that I belonged to the most expensive tennis complex around, paying something like $8,000 a year to play for a couple of hours a week over a period of eight weeks. (We spent the summers in Connecticut, so I only played for five weekends in late May and June, and three in September.) But, I added philosophically, for that $8,000 Riverdale threw in my children's education free.

    For a $20 entry fee to the 65's tournament, I presume that at least a new can of balls will be furnished and that I'll get a towel without paying an additional quarter or whatever.

    Thinking of towels, I wonder whether exquisite etiquette will be the rule after a match. After all, much more important tournaments, especially the one involving spry youngsters in the 45's

division, will be going on simultaneously. Will they come into the
locker room sweating just about as profusely as I, and bow and
wave me to the few showerheads, saying "You first, good sir"?
I rather doubt it, so I think I'll take along my warm-up sweat
clothes to wear while I wait, and hope they don't use up all the
hot water.

February 25
It is now just a little more than a week before my rendezvous with
destiny, and I must admit that I'm starting to wonder about it
again, having more or less put it out of my mind this past month.
Luckily, I ran into an old friend today who used to be an outstanding senior player. He has now reached an age when he has hung up
his racquet as far as competitive events are concerned, but he still
maintains a lively interest in the sport, even officiating now and
then as umpire, or linesman, at important events. I told him what I
planned to do and, since he knows the calibre of my game, asked
him if I was in over my head. He answered this way:

"As far as winning or being a finalist or even a semifinalist, you
are. There will be at least three or four, and very possibly more,
sixty-five-year-olds in that tournament who have made a career in
later life of becoming what they themselves would proudly admit
to being—tennis bums. There always are in any USTA tournament
of any standing. They are men who have retired, or are rich enough
and important enough to take time off and get in some play every
day, and then there are a number of teaching professionals, too,
who compete in senior tournaments.

"It's sort of a retirement career, and a nice one if you like to play
tennis that much. I know—I was one of them. I would travel far
from home, to the South, the Midwest, once even to the West
Coast, to play in these things. Between travel expenses, putting up
for the better part of a week at a hotel or motel, and everything
else, I was often spending several hundred dollars in order to try to
get a Senior ranking that nobody except myself would ever notice,
or try to win a silver-plated cup that retailed for ten or twenty

dollars in a shop and was worth absolutely nothing in a pawnshop.

"For some years now tennis has been a big-money game. People who happened to know I had done well in some tournament or other used to ask me, 'How much did you win?', having just read that Laver or Connors or someone had pulled down a hundred thousand or more for a single match. My invariable reply was something like 'It cost me $467.18.'

"So you *are* going to find real jocks who were always as good or better than you ever were and who have concentrated on playing with intensity ever since they were forty-five and eligible to tour both the winter circuit and the summer events. If you have to face one of them, he will wipe you off the court. Len Hartman, who is running your tournament, and is himself over sixty-five, will undoubtedly play, and he's an example. Len was an outstanding college player at Columbia, and a great all-around athlete at all sports, including being an all–Ivy League basketball star. When he was in the sixties age category a few years ago, Len entered the National Indoor sixties championship and went to the finals. But the USTA didn't rank him at all that year, because he hadn't played in enough tournaments. That annoyed him enough that he inaugurated and got recognition for this New York State Seniors affair that he now runs every year at his own place, the Parade Grounds. That way, unless he breaks an ankle, he knows he's going to get a high New York State ranking at the very least.

"So forget any roseate dreams of glory you may have experienced about winning. Len, and probably several others, will be out of your class. On the other hand, there could well be a number of hopefuls, more or less of your level, and perhaps you can have some fun before you're demolished."

Thank you, old friend. I am glad to know the score. We who are about to die salute you.

March 7
This is D day, but it's the F train on the Independent subway line that will take me out to the Fort Hamilton Parkway station in

Brooklyn, a 35-minute run from my Rockefeller Center office if a train ever comes along, they tell me. Considering the four-block walk to the courts after that, and the time I'll need to change into tennis gear and look at the draw, I'd better allow an hour and a quarter.

The train does arrive, and somewhat to my amazement and dismay, every car is jammed to the gills with people. It's as crowded as if it were the 5:30 rush hour. Where *can* all these people be going, toward Brooklyn, at the noon hour? Most of them are certainly too young to be playing in the Seniors, and besides, I seem to be the only one carrying a tennis racquet. Well, at least I don't have to expend much energy standing up, because I'm held erect by the solid press of flanking human bodies on all sides, until we reach the Jay Street–Borough Hall stop in Brooklyn. That, for some unknown reason, is where everyone is getting off, and I am able to sink gratefully into a seat.

At Fort Hamilton Parkway I emerge into the open air and ask directions of the first person I meet. Unlike the people who do not know, but give you directions anyway, this woman doesn't hesitate a moment and points me in the right direction for the Parade Grounds without even pausing to think about it. I arrive, check in, and look at the draw sheets.

It is clear that my old friend knew what he was talking about. Already I see some familiar faces among those dressed in tennis gear, and on the draw-sheet board I spot some very recognizable and scary names. Top seeded among the 45's, for example, is Bob Barker, who has been dominating metropolitan Senior play for some time and is still good enough to make just about any tennis player in the world work up a substantial sweat. Second-seeded in that group is Jim Gilchrist, former Australian Davis Cup squad member; Jim, who is now actually 55 years old, is doubling up in two tournaments, the 45's and 55's, being seeded number one in the latter. I don't know Bob Schwartz, the number two seeded player in the 55's, but he must be mighty good because I see he is seeded in front of Steve Ogilvy, who is placed at number three. I know Steve's reputation only too well. He was a standout college star at Princeton and for the past several decades has been a terror in any New England tournament he entered. I don't know if he was ever quite good enough to compete in the Nationals, but if he wasn't, he was mighty close to it. Anyway, here he is good enough to be doubling up, too, playing in the 60's, where he is seeded number one. Just under him at number two is the first black player in this country to make a name for himself, Dr. Reggie Weir, who played in the Nationals years before anyone ever heard of Arthur Ashe. Len Hartman, who is also doubling up, is seeded number three here, and in the only division for which I rally have eyes—the 65's—Len is the number-two seed. Heavens! Who can be number one? The answer is Ed Tarangioli, who as a senior seems not to have lost to *anyone* within living memory. If I ever have to run up against him I will need a rifle, not a tennis racquet.

At the number-three spot in the 65's is Harold Meltzner, about whom I know nothing, but I am fated to learn. Last year he was ranked number three in the 60's division in the East, but now he has turned 65 and has moved up to the older and presumably weaker division. Not much encouragement for me there. Finally, the number four seeded player turns out to be that wily and talented teaching professional, Sam Shore, who runs his own prestigious tennis club in Port Washington and who lives and breathes tennis.

I don't recognize any of the other names, including that of my first-round opponent, which may or may not be encouraging. After all, no one here is going to recognize my name, either. I wander back to the locker room to get dressed.

Once there, the immediate fancy that strikes me as I glance around the room and take a deep breath is that when I get back to my office I should telephone my broker and see what he thinks about investing in Ace bandages, Bauer & Black thigh, ankle, and arm braces, leather tennis elbow and knee supports, liniments and ointments like Ben-Gay, and vitamin pills. I would have estimated that the world's supply might be crowded into that small room, but as I thoughtfully pulled on my own Futuro elastic calf support, I was brooding about how big a business this might really be out there on the Senior tennis circuit. I'm not sure that OPEC would be in the same league.

There are only just enough entries in the 65's tournament to fill a draw of 16, and owing to some scheduling confusion in the other divisions, certain of the day's matches, including mine, have to be postponed a couple of hours. The same is true of another nonentity's match, involving a chap who, like me, is dressed and ready to go. We don't want to hang around for nothing for that long, and there is a free court, so we agree to play a meaningless warm-up "professional set," first man to win nine games is the winner.

He is tall and rangy, with powerful ground strokes that often sail over the baseline, so he obviously, and probably sensibly, rushes the net on virtually every point. But these are not effective tactics for him against me, because two of the strongest points of my game are good passing shots and quite a deadly lob, when it's working. Those were enough to enable me to wipe him out 9–1, without breathing hard, and even though it didn't count for anything, I felt considerably more relaxed. Len Hartman had been right in his terse guess that I am at least as good as some entries. There is one entrant who isn't nearly as good as I, and maybe there will be more. After all, where there's smoke, there's fire. But when my actual first-round opponent shows up and reveals himself, he inspires mixed emotions in my breast.

On the one hand, he is two inches shorter than I, and when I claim to be 5'8" I am exaggerating by almost an inch. And his snow-white hair and general appearance make him appear to be a possible candidate for a *real* veterans' affair—the veterans of the Spanish-American War. Still, he tells me he is currently the teaching professional at a metropolitan tennis club. Even more chilling is the fact that his bag contains no less than four racquets, and his warm-up suit, T-shirt, and shorts are emblazoned with an embroidered patch in two colors that reads USLTA. Admittedly, that tabs him as somewhat passé, regardless of whether he's in the 65's tournament or not, since the United States Lawn Tennis Association changed into the USTA a couple of years ago when they dropped the word "Lawn" from the name of the organization. Still, it is a nice piece of gamesmanship, calculated to throw terror into an opponent. Somewhere, somehow, someplace, this fellow seems to have won his letters!

Our time arrives, and we receive a new can of balls, towels, and even an umpire. My opponent turns out to be pretty steady and has a nasty slice both on his serve and his forehand, but I have more pace and can run rings around him, so I win very handily in two straight sets. He takes only four games from me, and at one stage I run off eleven straight points. I would like to put aside a sneaking suspicion I have that he might have been my father's roommate in college. I don't want to mar the wonderful reality that I am now a quarter-finalist in the New York State Senior 65's. To add to my pleasure, the subway train I take home is almost empty and I not only get one seat but positively sprawl over two or three while I work out the *Times* crossword puzzle, which I've saved from the morning since I couldn't raise my arm to work on it on the trip out. There's a copy of the *News* and one of the *Post*, too, that have been left behind by other riders, so I work those puzzles as well before we get back to Rockefeller Center. Not a record performance, it's true, but good.

March 9

Yesterday was a day off, but today here I am again, hoping that nothing too important is happening at the office, and ready to play my quarter-final match.

First, the good news. I am not playing either Ed Tarangioli or Len Hartman.

Now for the bad news. I am playing against Harold Meltzner. Well, it had to be one of the four seeded players at this stage, so here we are.

Harold turns out to be an extremely pleasant opponent in every respect, except that he never makes an unforced error, a talent for which I myself am know in my circles, but Meltzner is definitely my master. Actually, I play just about my best, and I win two games in the first set and three in the second, but the match isn't really as close as even those scores might indicate. For he is solidly in command all the way, jumping off to a two- or three-game lead at the start of both sets and then holding a comfortable lead throughout. Several of the games he wins go to deuce, or even to my ad, but Harold wins all the important points he has to. That's something I can usually do in my own hacker's league, but Harold is one who can do it to me. We had five spectators seated courtside on camp chairs, none of whom I knew except Mrs. Meltzner, whom Harold introduced to me just before we began, and who sat and knitted throughout the match. Like Madame DeFarge.

Still, I haven't made a spectacle of myself, and after our match, over soft drinks, he confirmed what my old friend had told me the previous month. Meltzner was not a truly serious player, although always a good one, before he turned 45. At that point in his life he had the means and the inclination to go in for Senior competitive tennis in a serious way, and since then he has played practically every day of his life, except when acts of God intervened. He slaps me on the back as we say good-bye and tells me I have a good, solid game, but that I had started 20 years too late if I expected to get anywhere as a Senior tennis bum.

Do you care about the outcome of the tournament? It went according to form in the two semi-finals, with Tarangioli beating Shore, and Hartman beating Meltzner. Of course, I had been hoping that Meltzner would go all the way, which would have made me look better, but Len beat him by just about the same scores as Harold had beaten me. Then, perhaps inspired by the fact that he had conquered the conquerer of Schwed, Len Hartman upset Tarangioli in the final in straight sets.

I traveled home on the subway for the last time (until next year, anyway) well satisfied. I must concede that I can never rival Len Hartman and be a famous athlete at 65, but I'm good enough at least to compete for fun. And that's good enough so that I don't have to be a gardener.